Brian Wynne

The Tuberous Begonia

Its history and cultivation

Brian Wynne

The Tuberous Begonia
Its history and cultivation

ISBN/EAN: 9783337011802

Printed in Europe, USA, Canada, Australia, Japan

Cover: Foto ©ninafisch / pixelio.de

More available books at **www.hansebooks.com**

THE
TUBEROUS BEGONIA,

ITS HISTORY AND CULTIVATION.

Illustrated.

By Contributors to "The Gardening World."

Edited by B. Wynne, F.R.H.S.,
Manager of "The Gardening World," Member of the Floral Committee of the Royal Horticultural Society, Honorary Member of the Cercle d'Arboriculture de Belgique, &c.

London:
Gardening World Office, 17, Catherine Street, Strand, W.C.

1888.

H. M. POLLETT & Co.,
HORTICULTURAL AND GENERAL STEAM PRINTERS,
FANN STREET, LONDON, E.C.

PREFACE.

The Proprietors of The Gardening World having decided to issue a series of popular books on subjects directly connected with gardening, and which, while published at popular prices, shall be of an essentially practical and useful character, we selected as the subject for the first volume of the series the Tuberous-rooted Begonia, first, on account of its remarkably popular character as a garden flower, and secondly, because we felt there was a want of a useful guide to its cultivation and further improvement. As to how far in the present treatise we have met that want, we must leave the generous flower-loving public to decide.

While aiming in the main to be practical, we have endeavoured to give some additional interest to the work by recording so much of the history of the modern Begonia as we have been able to glean, and though very imperfect as this portion of our subject undoubtedly is, we would fain hope that it may prove of some value as a basis for a record more completely worthy of the subject. For many of the facts relating to the history of the earlier varieties, and for the whole of the illustrations of the same, we are indebted to the courtesy of Messrs. James Veitch and Sons, to whom the honour belongs of having laid the foundation of a race of plants which Mr. Laing and others have brought to such marvellous perfection. To Messrs. Cannell and Sons our thanks are also due for the use of several of the woodcuts which we have selected to illustrate some of the modern types of the flower; and we desire also to tender our best thanks to Mr. W. E. Gumbleton—one of the first amateurs to recognise the merits of "the coming flower"— for many valuable hints; and to Mr. B. C. Ravenscroft, for the cultural articles which constitute the greater portion of the work.

B. W.

July, 1888.

TABLE OF CONTENTS.

———

                                                  PAGE

Introduction 1

A BRIEF SKETCH OF THE BEGONIA FAMILY.

Number of species—Essential characters of the genus—Interesting exceptions to the general characteristics—Behaviour under cultivation—The genus Hildebrandia 10

HISTORY OF THE TUBEROUS BEGONIA.

The species from which the modern race has been obtained—The first garden Hybrid—List of Hybrids raised by Messrs. Veitch—Hybrids raised by Messrs. O'Brien, Bull, Sutton and others—The Forest Hill Strain—The Swanley Collection—The Continental Seedlings—The introducer of the Tuberous Begonias 14

PROPAGATION OF THE BEGONIA.

By Seeds—Preparing the Pans and sowing the Seeds—Treatment after germination—Transplanting into Boxes or Trays—Potting on and Subsequent Treatment—By Cuttings—Leaf Cuttings 34

CULTIVATION OF THE BEGONIA IN POTS.

Selecting and starting the Tubers—Compost for the first Potting, Watering, &c.—The Second Potting—A few more words about Compost—Open-Stages, Watering, Damping, &c.—The Third Potting, Temperature, Ventilation, &c.—Treatment when in bloom—After Flowering 46

DOUBLE-FLOWERING BEGONIAS.

The march of improvement—The variety of form—The erect-flowering section—Potting and Composts, &c.—Hints on Propagation 56

TABLE OF CONTENTS.

BEGONIAS FOR EXHIBITION.

Suitable Composts—Heat, Moisture and Shading—Feeding with Artificial Manure—Hints on Packing for Travelling 67

BEGONIAS FOR LATE AUTUMN FLOWERING.

Their early treatment—Management in Autumn 71

THE NEW RACE OF WINTER-FLOWERING BEGONIAS.

Begonia socotrana—Characteristics of the first crosses—The first Hybrid raised—The latest varieties 74

BEGONIAS FOR BEDDING-OUT.

Small *v.* large plants—Starting the Tubers—Preparing the Beds and planting—Arrangement of the plants—Suitable plants for combinations—Preserving the Tubers in winter—Fibrous-rooted varieties 79

SEED SAVING AND HYBRIDISATION.

The properties of a Single Begonia—The points of a Double Begonia—How and when to manipulate the blooms—Natural fertilisation—Artificial fertilisation—Marking the Crosses—Gathering the Seeds—Selecting the flowers for crossing—Hybridising double flowers—The first Double varieties 86

THE BEST FORM OF BEGONIA HOUSE 100
SELECTIONS OF VARIETIES 102

LIST OF ILLUSTRATIONS.

PORTRAITS.

	PAGE
The late Mr. RICHARD PEARCE ... ... *Frontispiece*	
Mr. JOHN LAING, Forest Hill	25
Mr. HENRY CANNELL, Swanley	29

SPECIES AND VARIETIES OF BEGONIAS.

Species printed in italics.

	PAGE
B. Acme ...	35
B. *boliviensis* ...	15
B. Camellia ...	89
B. Chelsoni ...	33
B. *Davisii* ...	21
B. Emperor ...	37
B. Felix Crousse ...	59
B. Glow ...	61
B. intermedia ...	31
B. John Heal ...	77
B. Mr. Poë ...	45
B. M. Truffaut ...	65
B. Queen of Whites ...	39
B. Queen Victoria ...	27
B. *rosæflora* ...	19
B. Rosamonde ...	63
B. Rose Céleste ...	87
B. *socotrana* ...	75
B. Sedeni ...	23
B. *Veitchii* ...	17
B. virginalis ...	57

The Tuberous Begonia,

ITS HISTORY AND CULTIVATION.

INTRODUCTION.

THE Tuberous-rooted Begonia—so called after M. Begon, a French botanist—though for some years subsequent to its introduction into this country in its original form but little esteemed, except perhaps to some extent as a curiosity, has of late years developed, under cultivation, so many valuable qualities, has proved itself to be possessed of so extraordinary a capability for improvement in almost every respect, and consequently is annually gaining in popularity by such long and rapid strides, that little doubt can be entertained that in the immediate future it will be cultivated in numbers approaching, if not absolutely equalling, those to which the Zonal Pelargonium has already attained. A duration of flowering extending continuously over a period of five or six months, and a range of colour embracing every imaginable shade of white, rose, pink, red, scarlet, crimson, lake, orange, and yellow, combined with the richest and most delicate tints, are no mean advantages to start with. And when to these are added a nearly perfect adaptability to almost any kind of culture—whether planted out-of-doors, or grown in pots, boxes or baskets, in the open air or under glass, with artificial heat or without, the power of withstanding apparently uninjured the extremes of wet and stormy weather, or of tropical heat and drought, a hardiness enabling the roots to endure uninjured in the open ground the severity of ordinary English winters, except perhaps in cold or wet soils—an unequalled capacity for being stored in large numbers without the aid of glass, and in a very small space—and, above all, the capability of being improved in every point that constitutes a first-class decorative subject to an extent up to the present time almost incredible, and still far from being fathomed or determined, as well as an extraordinary profuseness and persistence of bloom, the flowers in most cases being also remarkable for size and showiness—who can say what future may be in store for such a plant, or what other denizen of our gardens and greenhouses can lay or substantiate a claim to so many advantages?

With the single exception of the Zonal Pelargonium there is no other plant, in the entire range of exotics, that can compare with the Begonia, either in regard to its capability for producing a gorgeous display of rich and varied colour, when grown in masses, or as a thoroughly useful and easily-cultivated decorative subject. Anyone who has visited the show houses of Messrs. John Laing and Sons, at Forest Hill, or of Messrs. Cannell and Sons, at Swanley, when in the height of perfection, will readily admit the former proposition; and those who attempt the culture of this plant, under conditions at all suitable, whether indoors or out, will very shortly agree to the latter, if they have not already done so.

In our opinion, nothing in the entire floral treasury can possibly surpass in effect a mass or large houseful of the choicest varieties of Zonal Pelargonium, both single and double, when skilfully grown in pure air, and just in perfection; but a collection of modern Begonias, under similar circumstances, will run them very close indeed, even as regards the production of large and dense masses of rich colour; while in quaintness and variety of form, habit, and colour, the Begonia might fairly be awarded the palm. Undeniably the Zonal Pelargonium is possessed of a few advantages that the Begonia lacks. For instance, the former will, under favourable conditions, continue to bloom throughout the winter, or, indeed, at any season of the year, and is therefore valuable as affording brightness, or a supply of flowers for cutting, at a time when bloom of any kind is scarce and welcome; while, though the Tuberous Begonia may, by starting the tubers early in the year, and growing them in a genial warmth, be got into flower by the month of May, or even April, and by the use of late-potted seedlings, or plants taken up from the open ground, be induced to prolong their season of beauty up to about Christmas-tide, yet, during the three or four months between these times, the roots demand a season of rest, and we must for the time be content to dispense with their presence. The new race of winter-flowering Begonias, however, which has been obtained by crossing Begonia socotrana with some of the summer-flowering varieties, promises ere long to give a plant that will carry on the flowering season right through the winter.

Again, the blooms of the Zonal Pelargonium — especially of the double-flowering forms — are undeniably much better adapted for cutting, and more particularly when the flowers have to be packed, or to travel any distance, and therefore become a more saleable commodity. At the same time, Begonia blooms, either single or double, are considerably more suitable for cutting, and useful when cut, than is generally imagined, and if they can be used on the spot, or very carefully carried, are really very valuable and effective for this purpose, and last a considerable time in water; but the delicate waxy petals are soon bruised and disfigured by any rough handling. The erect-flowering varieties are exceedingly useful in making up choice bouquets, and in specimen glasses, button-holes, etc., while the drooping kinds come in admirably in filling epergnes, and other methods of table decoration.

INTRODUCTION.

The propagation of the Begonia, either by means of cuttings or from seed, is a delicate and tedious or uncertain operation, compared with the ease with which Pelargonium cuttings may be rooted in quantity by the merest tyro. On the other hand, Pelargoniums must be wintered in a properly constructed and efficiently heated glasshouse, must receive daily attention, and occupy a large amount of space; whereas, in the case of Begonias, all such care and expense is entirely unnecessary, and a hundred—nay, a thousand Begonia roots may be stored in the space occupied by a dozen Pelargoniums; and more than this, any out-of-the-way place or odd corner, such as under a greenhouse stage, or in a shed, or kitchen cupboard even—provided frost is thoroughly excluded —will afford all the accommodation they need. Throughout the whole winter all the attention they require is to be looked over two or three times, picking out any decayed tubers, and seeing that they are neither in danger of rotting from damp, nor of shrivelling from excessive dryness. In warm and sheltered localities, or on light, dry soils, the roots may even be allowed to remain in the ground all winter with perfect safety, if well established. Even severe frost will not injure them under such conditions, if not too near the surface, though in any case it is advisable to cover each plant or row with a few inches depth of ashes, or coco-nut fibre refuse.

The improvements that have been effected in this flower, by means of skilful and persevering hybridisation, since it first attracted attention, are simply marvellous, and undeniably no other flowering plant in cultivation has made such rapid and wonderful strides, or undergone such remarkable changes for the better in so short a time, as Tuberous Begonias. Indeed, anyone who had not watched the progress that has year by year and step by step been made, would scarcely credit that the huge circular and leathery blooms of to-day, with their glowing or dazzling colours, could by any possibility have been derived from the poor pale, flimsy, and long-petalled flowers that the Begonias of ten or twelve years ago could produce. It must, however, be admitted that some of the first seedlings raised in this country, such as "Vesuvius," "Acme," "Emperor," etc., were, and still are, remarkably floriferous in character—much more so than the majority of the large-flowering varieties that have been more recently produced—as well as being more bushy in growth, and possessed of great hardiness and very vigorous constitutions, when compared with some of the highly-bred productions of the present day. Indeed, the varieties above named, with a few others of the same class, are still retained by first-class cultivators, who endeavour, by crossing them with varieties possessing larger and better formed flowers and brighter colours, to obtain a race of hybrids, suitable for out-of-door cultivation, which will combine the good qualities of both strains. As a matter of fact, this object has already to a great extent been attained, and there are now a number of single varieties bearing fairly large and brightly-coloured flowers in almost, if not quite, as great profusion as old-fashioned kinds to which we have referred, and also possessing such vigorous constitutions as to enable them to be propagated from cuttings, perfectly true to type, on a large scale and with great success. This is saying a great deal, for nineteen out of twenty Begonias deteriorate so rapidly when increased in this manner as to become in a short time almost worthless. But even were this rule absolute, we can always fall back upon seedlings, which have far more vigour than plants raised from cuttings; and it is now a noticeable and proved fact that seed saved from a distinct and strongly characterised class of plants, such as the above, will produce a large proportion possessing all the desirable qualities of the parents, combined in varying degree; while a judicious system of selection will eliminate any stragglers, and ensure the continuation, and probably the advancement, of the type.

The value of Begonias as bedding-out plants, though beginning to be recognized by a few, is very far indeed from being appreciated to a tithe of its actual extent. The result of employing these elegant plants in this capacity is, when carried out in a tolerably judicious and suitable manner, always so highly satisfactory in every respect, that their general adoption for the purposes of the decoration of the flower garden is only a matter of time. Indeed, they have already gained a considerable footing in many districts where a fair trial has been given them; and among these may be mentioned such widely separated localities as some parts of Devonshire (where Begonias succeed amazingly well, and give little or no trouble), the Highlands of Scotland, and the extreme eastern counties of England. In Devonshire very good Begonias are now to be seen in a high degree of perfection, not only in the gardens of the rich, and those who take a strong interest in the advancement of horticulture, but in many cottage and farm-house gardens as well, where they seem to be equally at home, and equally appreciated. In some of the eastern counties, again, these Begonias are made a speciality in many gardens; while in Scotland, among other places, they have been introduced, and are now extensively cultivated with the greatest success in the gardens of Drummond Castle in Perthshire, at New Tarbat in Ross-shire, and at Culloden in Inverness-shire; and also in several instances in the Carse o'Gowrie.

Seedlings raised in good time, and planted out early in June, though they do not come into full bloom until rather late, and attain no great size, make a fine display of bright and varied colour during August, September, and even October of the same year as well, when the latter month assumes the calm and genial character which in many seasons renders it almost the most enjoyable month of the year—at least in country places, and to the lover of "rural sights and sounds." In support of this fact may be instanced the appearance of Messrs. John Laing and Son's nursery beds, the main quarter of which this year contains 112,000 seedlings. Tubers one, two, or more years old are, however, naturally more satisfactory than seedlings, as they not only commence flowering much earlier in the season, but form much more floriferous and bushy, as well as larger, plants. The single-flowering varieties are undoubtedly much more suitable for out-of-door decoration than the doubles, the blooms of which, especially in the case of the more improved kinds, are not produced with sufficient rapidity, nor remain so long on the plant; so that they become to some extent disfigured by the weather before their natural span of life is nearly completed. Either in masses of harmoniously-arranged or contrasted colours, as single specimens (as a centre in small beds, or in other similar positions), for which rather large plants are naturally best adapted, or dotted here and there with more or less regard to uniformity in mixed, or even herbaceous borders (in which position they afford an excellent contrast to plants of other character or habit), the Tuberous Begonia is simply an invaluable subject, and invariably creates a fine effect. The more commonly cultivated varieties with drooping flowers are exceedingly graceful and admirable; but a class has recently been produced, by careful selection, of stiffer habit, bearing flowers held more or less erect, which of course present themselves more fully to the eye of a spectator than plants possessing only pendulous blooms can do.

By far the most valuable characteristic of the Begonia, when employed as a bedding-out plant, is its remarkable power of withstanding the influence of extremes of weather and climate. In this respect it possesses a great advantage over the Pelargonium, which, however brilliant and beautiful it may be when in good condition, needs very special weather to enable it to develope its capabilities to the full, when planted out of doors in our uncertain English climate; while the Begonia pursues the even tenor of its way all through the season, come sunshine or shower, heat or cold; and not only looks up to all appearance refreshed and invigorated, instead of bruised and battered, after a storm of wind and rain, but seems equally unaffected by a long period of tropical heat and drought, provided only that its roots are working in a stratum of rich and comparatively moist earth below the surface. The Begonia is also devoid of the serious tendency of the Zonal Pelargonium to "run to leaf" in wet and sunless seasons. As long as growth continues it produces a truss of bloom at every joint, which never fails to expand if the temperature is moderately high. Sudden changes from hot to cold weather alone seem to have an injurious effect, sometimes causing a portion of the buds to drop before expanding. In the cold wet summers we experienced four or five years ago, Begonias outside looked as bright and fresh as possible all through the season; and again during the intense heats of the last summer the plants seemed literally to luxuriate in the tropical blaze, and flowered with exceptional freedom, so long as there was a supply of moisture about the roots, causing the beds to produce the effect of solid sheets of dazzling bloom.

The scarlet and crimson shades, which naturally predominate in a good class of these plants, are, of course, more effective, either in the open air or under glass, than the quieter and more subdued colours. Many of the varieties now in cultivation, of varying tints of these bright or deep reds, are so dazzlingly brilliant in hue as quite to equal, if not surpass, the colours of the finest Zonal Pelargoniums in existence, and a mass of such flowers viewed under the influence of bright sunshine presents a broad effect of rich and solid colour as can scarcely be equalled by any other means. Again, the white-flowered varieties, which are now exceedingly pure in colour, and have been vastly improved not only in habit but in every other respect, compared with what they were a very few years ago—the delicate pink shades, the purplish-crimsons, with other fine tints, and, above all, the more or less pure yellow blooms—are a welcome addition to our parterres and borders, and will generally be found to flower as freely as the commoner red and scarlet sections.

Among many other arrangements one of the most taking combinations consists of a careful, but seemingly careless and natural, grouping of several varieties of ornamental-foliaged sub-tropical subjects, with a few Fuchsias or other flowering plants, and Begonias of various colours. For instance, take a few plants each of Castor-Oil (Ricinus), Cannas, Japanese Maize, Perilla, Amaranthus, Abutilons, and Nicotianas, with perhaps a Dracæna or Palm or two, and a few Fuchsias, yellow Calceolarias or the like, and arrange them carefully in a circular or other suitably-shaped bed, with a dozen or so of Begonias of various colours and height, some large old specimens being placed among the taller occupants of the centre or back portion of the bed or border, with the smaller and dwarfer examples towards the front or edge; and if the whole is well done and the colours, etc., judiciously contrasted, a most beautiful effect will be produced. It is not desirable to arrange the various plants so as to produce a too-regular gradation in height, for a much better result is attained by allowing here and there a tall Begonia or Fuchsia to rise well above dwarfer Amaranthus, Calceolarias, or the like; or a graceful Dracæna or Grevillea here and there to break the monotony of a group or ring of low-growing Begonias. This portion of the subject will, however, be dealt with more fully in another chapter.

In filling hollows in rustic stumps of trees, or ornamental flower-stands, vases, etc., these Begonias are exceedingly useful and effective, usually flourishing remarkably in such positions. As a rule, single varieties are most suitable for this and kindred purposes, and where the plant is on a level with, or above the average level of the eye, drooping-flowered kinds give the best effect. For hanging baskets, either in or out of doors, they are equally well adapted, and in this case only those of drooping habit should be employed. Some of the free-growing and profusely-flowering doubles are very effective as basket plants in the greenhouse or conservatory. Wherever Begonias are employed in any of the above methods in the open air, it is note-worthy that the situation can scarcely be too sunny to suit them, if only the roots are kept well supplied with moisture; whereas, under glass, they seem to endure but a very moderate amount of summer sunshine without injury. At the same time, plants in the open air, especially when on elevated positions, will succeed to perfection in a shaded situation, if the shade is not too heavy or dense.

Begonias raised from seed do not, as a rule, exceed about 1 foot in height the first year, if planted out of doors in a fairly open situation. The second season they will probably attain a height of about 18 inches, or, perhaps, rather more, and will annually increase in size up to about the fourth year, when they may attain a height of 3 feet or so. These figures may be taken subject to considerable variation, according to the character of the individual plant, the situation, and general treatment. When grown under glass, the above heights will probably be exceeded considerably, especially should light or ventilation not be sufficiently abundant.

The fact that no kind of insect-pest seems to have any particular predilection for the Begonia is a point greatly in its favour, and one which will go a long way to ensure its popularity, as it naturally renders its culture so much simpler, and often less expensive. During an experience of some years we have never seen these plants affected by anything but a few small aphides, and on still fewer occasions by a little thrip on the under side of the leaves. In every case this was distinctly traceable to neglect or bad management in some form, and the insects are always easily removeable. Red-spider never seems to touch them, and so far only one kind of disease is known to affect them, which is of a fungoid character, and causes the stems or leaves to assume a brown scaly appearance, and to become very brittle. This, however, is directly caused by too high a temperature, with an insufficient amount of ventilation, and in some cases assisted by a want of cleanliness in the house, and a lack of the necessary amount of moisture at the root. Plants in the open air, as well as those grown in a cool and airy structure, are never affected by it. We believe this affection to be identical, or nearly so, with the Gloxinia disease, and it exercises a similarly crippling effect upon the growth of the plant once it has obtained a good hold. The only cure is a preparation of sulphur; but this seems to be ineffectual after a certain stage has been reached.

The double-flowering forms of the Tuberous-rooted Begonia are, in their way, equally valuable with the single varieties, and quite as deserving of attention; indeed, for some purposes even more so. They are not as a rule so well adapted for out-door cultivation; but when well grown in a suitable glass structure are even more beautiful and unique than the singles. On the whole, the constitution of the double kinds of Begonia is not so robust as that of the singles, though great improvements have recently been made in this respect; and, like most other double-flowering plants, they require greater care and skill to bring them to the highest state of perfection than the single forms, and in some points, slightly different treatment. On this account we have thought it best to treat of this class in a separate chapter (*see* p. 56). When really well done, in good health, and in suitable quarters, these double flowers remain in beauty longer than those of almost any other plant, Orchids alone excepted. We have frequently noticed blooms on some plants of double-flowering Begonias to last and remain in good condition on the plant for at least three or four weeks, and in some cases for even a longer time than this. The buds, particularly of the very large and fully double varieties, open very slowly, expanding by often barely perceptible degrees from day to day; and when fully developed, they do not, as the single kinds are rather apt to do, drop off unexpectedly, but remain upon the stalk until petal by petal they wither away.

The improvements that have been effected since their first introduction are even more extraordinary in this section than in the case of the single forms. We can distinctly remember some of the first double Begonias that were raised. Certainly they were far from beautiful, and it can scarcely be wondered that for a long time so little attention was paid to them. The blooms were then about 1½ or barely 2 inches in diameter, mostly only semi-double or little more, and consisting of a few narrow-pointed flimsy petals of a dull red, or sickly pink colour, while the habit of the plant was still worse, the growth being in some cases a yard long or thereabout, with small and scanty foliage, and often crowned by no more than one or two forlorn-looking blooms—a spectacle of pity. Still, they were double, and bit by bit have been improved in size, shape, colour, and in the number of petals, as well as in habit and growth, until at the present time a well-grown double Begonia, of a really good variety, is about as beautiful an object as the most ardent horticulturist or amateur could desire to behold, or as could be met with in the whole range of floral beauty. The very largest double blooms are often of some shade of pink, frequently with a white centre, though the largest blooms are generally of a soft bright red. The double whites, if pure, are generally of only a moderate size, though many of the blush and cream-coloured flowers are large, and some blooms among the rich red and crimson shades are now of immense size, the largest being found among the pæony-flowered section. Double yellows up to the present time have been comparatively scarce, but fine new varieties are now making their appearance in greater numbers.

Among the double Begonias, we have now whites as snowy and pure in colour, as double, and nearly as perfect in form as a Camellia (*see* p. 89), an infinite number of shades of blush, rose, pink, orange, and many other similar shades, as well as rich scarlet and crimson flowers; and though in these darker shades we cannot quite equal the brilliant and glowing tints of some of the newest and best single varieties, yet the attainment of this perfection of colouring is only a matter of time. Most of the yellow and orange-coloured doubles have a decided tendency to produce erect flowers, much more so, we think, than those of any other shade. This peculiarity is also distinctly noticeable in the single kinds. These and other late productions in yellow-flowered doubles may be said to bring this section nearly on a level with the varieties of other and more common colours. As those we saw last year were mostly the produce of plants only a few months old, they will probably be much finer this season, for double Begonias do not, as a rule, do much more than show their character the first year, and it is on one and two-year-old plants that the largest and finest blooms are produced.

The Tuberous Begonia can unfortunately hardly be classed as a good town plant, smoky or impure air having too often the effect of causing the yet unopened or just expanding buds to drop off. Still, many of the more robust and free-flowering single varieties may be cultivated with a fair amount of success in all but the worst situations; and in most suburban gardens, where light and free air are tolerably abundant, very good results indeed are to be obtained by the exercise of a little care and skill. To all growers residing in or near large towns, however, we would strongly recommend the adoption of seedling plants in preference to named kinds, which require the most favourable conditions to ensure success. The double forms are even more susceptible of the effects of an impure atmosphere than the single kinds, and their culture should as a rule only be attempted where the surroundings are comparatively favourable—we mean as regards light, space, and absence of smoke. But to enable this flower to attain the full height of perfection, and develope all its grand and gorgeous capabilities, it is necessary to transport it to some fresh and open country place, where it can receive the benefit of a sweet and pure atmosphere, and clear and unobstructed light. Under these conditions it presents itself in quite a new aspect, and with even ordinary care developes a sturdiness and vigour, as well as extraordinary floriferousness, of the plant itself; and a size, brilliancy, and persistency of bloom and petal as to somewhat surprise those who have only seen or grown it under less favourable circumstances, and at once to settle any doubts as to its rightful claim to a place in the very first rank of decorative plants.

A BRIEF SKETCH OF THE BEGONIA FAMILY.

THE Begonia family consists of some 350 or more species, which are being added to from time to time as new discoveries are made. It consists of two genera, but with one exception all are species of Begonia, and are distributed through tropical America, Asia (chiefly on the other side of the Ganges), and in tropical and sub-tropical South Africa; in all of which countries they grow in great abundance. Few are found in the islands of the Pacific Ocean, and, so far as is at present known, no species are indigenous to Australia.

The Begonias, as a natural group or family, stand isolated as it were from even the nearest of their allies in the vegetable kingdom, forming a very characteristic and readily recognised class of plants, with succulent or sub-shrubby stems, reduced to a short fleshy tuber, as in the tuberous-rooted group, or have somewhat scandent or climbing stems, as in B. glaucophylla or B. fagifolia, which cling to a wall or other moist surface by means of numerous roots which they throw out. Their other characteristics consist of stipulate, generally ornamental leaves, mostly oblique at the base; irregular or unsymmetrical monœcious flowers, that is, there are male and female blooms on the same plant; numerous free or monadelphous stamens, that is, united in one bundle; and an inferior three—rarely two—four or many-celled ovary, with numerous minute seeds scattered over a very much enlarged entire or bifid placenta that projects into the cavity of the seed-vessel. The fruit is a trigonous or sometimes winged capsule, and rarely fleshy, resembling a berry. The nearest allies of this family are four species constituting the Datisca family, with which they agree in the structure of the seeds, ovary, and unisexual flowers. There is also a slight apparent affinity between the order and those of the Cucumber family, the Passion Flowers, and the Saxifrages.

THE ESSENTIAL CHARACTERS OF THE GENUS BEGONIA.

THESE are that the perianth is irregular, and usually, if not always, coloured like a corolla, consisting in the male flowers of four sepals in two series, rarely more or fewer; and in the female flowers of five spirally arranged, imbricating sepals. The stamens are numerous and free, or united into a more or less elongated bundle, and occupy the axis of the flower. The ovary is inferior, that is, wholly sunk in the receptacle or top of the flower stalk, which is adnate to it, so that the sepals appear to spring from the top of it; three—rarely one, two—four, or five-celled; styles equalling the cells in number, free or united at the base, and more or less deeply two-lobed or divided; placentas axile, rarely parietal. The three-angled or often winged fruit is a capsule opening at the angles or on the sides beneath the calyx, rarely baccate or fleshy, and not bursting. These characters are, however, exceedingly variable in different species, as might be expected in such an extensive genus; and the genus has been divided into forty-one genera by a German author, Klotzsch, but the characters are so inconstant in different members of various groups that the classification could not be retained. Alphonse de Candolle divided the genus into three, namely, Casparya, Begonia, and Mezierea, according as the fruit burst at the angles, at the sides, or had parietal placentas, respectively; but these characters are also too inconstant for the retention of such a classification. The sections and genera of those authors are, however, used in the *Genera Plantarum* for the purpose of grouping the various members of the genus in some intelligible and systematic way.

Interesting Exceptions to the General Characteristics.

There are some interesting exceptions to the above-mentioned botanical characters. In the section Begoniella, the sepals are united into a bell-shaped calyx, enclosing a definite number of stamens. The sepals are reduced to two in B. dipetala in both the male and female flowers, while several of the smaller-flowered species have the male flowers in this condition. The male blooms in B. octopetala vary with from six to nine sepals, resembling in no small measure the flowers of an Anemone, while the cordate-orbicular and lobed leaves serve to strengthen the illusion. The female flowers, as well as those of B. socotrana and others, have six sepals. The large placentas projecting into the cavity of the ovary are a marked feature of this, as well as some other orders, and they are entire as in B. socotrana, two-lobed or two-parted in others, and occasionally many-lobed. They project from the walls of the ovary, which is accordingly one-celled (as already mentioned), in the section Mezierea. Many species are remarkable for the production of adventitious buds and leaves from the surface of the stem or leaves themselves. As an instance of this erratic condition, B. phyllomaniaca may be mentioned, the stems of which may often be seen densely covered with small leaves.

Many species, as is well known to gardeners, may be propagated from leaves or cuttings of leaves. The old-fashioned B. Evansiana produces numerous bulbils in the axils of the upper leaves, by which it is regularly propagated in many a cottage window. B. gracilis Martiana, another tuberous-rooted species with showy flowers, also produces bulbils in vast numbers. In B. socotrana and the new race of winter-flowering garden forms partly derived from it, the bulbils are usually of large size and mostly confined to the base of the stem. B. socotrana occasionally flowers directly from these bulbils, on peduncles unaccompanied by leaves. The bulbils themselves consist of broad, overlapping pale green scales, which are the morphological equivalents of leaves. Economically the genus is not of much importance; but B. tuberosa and B. malabarica are used as potherbs in their native country.

The flowers or leaves, or both taken together, are often very showy, so that of the 350 known species it is not surprising that a large number of them have been introduced from time to time. Both in Britain and on the Continent especially the work of introduction continues to be prosecuted. B. nitida, which was brought from Jamaica in 1777, seems to have been the first introduction to this country, but up till 1800 only five species seem to have been in cultivation. Since then, till now, however, they have increased in number with greater or less rapidity, according to the zeal of cultivators or the fashion of the times. Several tuberous-rooted species have been introduced from time to time, but the advent of the six tuberous species from South America within comparatively recent years, and which are described in another chapter, has given a fresh impetus to their cultivation; and the immensely improved and numerous progeny that has been derived from them, now occupies a permanent position in the routine of culture in hundreds of gardens.

Although upwards of half of the 350 known species have been introduced, it will be germane to our purpose in a work like the present to group in sections those only in which we are specially concerned. B. boliviensis, introduced in 1864, belongs to the section Barya, which is characterised by the filaments being united, forming a long tassel-like column, and by the bifid placentas. Another species, B. monadelpha, having the same characters, does not seem to be in cultivation. The staminal column is a well-marked feature, and the sepals are also greatly elongated and narrow. B. Clarkei, B. Veitchii, B. rosæflora, B. Pearcei, and B. Davisii, all belong to the section Huszia, having free stamens, bifid placentas, and the stigmatic surfaces forming a papillose spiral line surrounding the branches of the styles. The first three mentioned have larger, rounder flowers and broader sepals than B. boliviensis.

Behaviour under Cultivation.

As might be expected, the size and shape of the flowers have been greatly altered by the effect of so much cross-breeding, hybridisation, and cultivation; but, from a botanical point of view, the most important and remarkable changes that have been accomplished relate to the doubling of the flowers, in which greater monstrosities and a more remarkable metamorphosis of parts occur than in those of any other natural order. The male flowers are those which most frequently become double, while the female ones on the same plant are usually single. Some of the earliest obtained double flowers were evidently derived from B. boliviensis, and were poor, ragged things, with scattered petaloid segments along an elongated axis. Since then, however, some of the grandest types of double flowers have been obtained from the same species, as may be witnessed in Messrs. John Laing and Sons' collection at Forest Hill. Some of the largest-flowered types more resemble a truss of a double scarlet Pelargonium than anything else. The sepals often remain of no great size, while the stamens become resolved into broad, flattened petaloid structures, bearing branches in their axils, and these branches terminate in little rosettes of similarly petaloid segments. The whole axis elongates before the flowers drop, and the secondary pedicels elongate so that the truss of the originally compact flower becomes a raceme of little flowers.

No less interesting is the phenomenon presented by the doubling of female flowers in many of the varieties. Not only does the normally inferior ovary become superior, but the carpels of which it is composed spread out flat, so that the placentas bearing myriads of small white ovules become exposed, while the upper part of the petaloid carpel may be scarlet, or of some other brilliant hue. No seeds can, of course, be developed by these monstrous doubles. A third remarkable type is represented by the variety Viridiflora, which is not the only instance of the kind by any means. The segments are shaped like ordinary leaves, being similarly lobed and toothed at the margin, and long before the flower drops they become quite green. Some single flowers even are crenated or fimbriated at the margin, resembling the leaves in this respect, although they retain their petaloid character and colour to the last. The narrow leaves of B. boliviensis are characteristic of most of Messrs. Laing's doubles.

The beautiful double varieties of Messrs. H. Cannell and Sons, Swanley, judging from the prevailing character of the broad leaves, and a slightly different habit, have evidently been derived from B. Veitchii, or others of the same type, such as B. rosæflora and B. Clarkei. In some of their doubles the true sepals are much longer than those of the central rosette, forming a cross-shaped guard. In others the whole flower consists of a number of rosettes collected together in one flower in a similar yet slightly different way to those mentioned above ; while a third type presents still more remarkable characters. A double flower primarily male has small outer or true sepals, while from the axils of two of these, two-stalked, single, female flowers are produced right and left of the originally male flower, so that there would seem to be practically no limit to variation.

The Genus Hildebrandia.

This is the only genus other than Begonia that belongs to the family. The flowers are regular or nearly so, consisting of five broadly ovate, acute sepals, and five small spathulate petals alternating with them. The stamens are numerous and free. The ovary is hemispherical, without wings, free at the apex, that is, partly superior and imperfectly five-celled, with five deeply two-lobed placentas, numerous small ovules, and five bilobed or forked styles. There are numerous small stalked glands springing from the sepals of the female flowers. The fruit is a capsule, bursting at the apex and between the sepals, similarly to that of the Mignonette. H. sandwichensis, a native of the Sandwich Islands, and the only species known, is a fleshy, hairy-stemmed, branching herb, with cordate-orbicular, lobed leaves, and axillary cymes of small whitish flowers. It is botanically interesting, but of no horticultural value.

HISTORY OF THE TUBEROUS BEGONIA.

ALL the varieties of the Tuberous Begonia now in existence, both single and double, are derived from six species — viz., B. boliviensis, B. Pearcei, B. Veitchii, B. rosæflora, B. Davisii, and B. Clarkei, and of these the five first-named were introduced into this country by Messrs. James Veitch and Sons, of Chelsea, and by them put into commerce.

Begonia boliviensis (*see* illustration, p. 15), which was the first of the series introduced by the Messrs. James Veitch and Sons, was collected by their traveller, Mr. Pearce, in Bolivia, and sent home in 1864. It was first exhibited in public at the International Horticultural Exhibition, held at Paris in May, 1867, and in the following year, 1868, it was put into commerce. In 1867 it was figured and described in the *Botanical Magazine*, t. 5657, as "a tuberous-rooted deciduous kind, attaining an average height of 2 feet. Its foliage is of a rather light green colour, of the 'fuschioides' character, and its small drooping flowers are of a bright cinnabar-scarlet colour." For a long time after its introduction, its small and thin-petalled flowers were much prized by horticulturists, though it was not perhaps showy enough to attract the attention of the general public.

Begonia Pearcei, the next to arrive in 1865, also came from Bolivia, having been collected at La Paz by Mr. Pearce, in whose honour it was fittingly named. This also is figured in the *Botanical Magazine*, t. 5545, and described as being "nearly allied in botanical character to B. cinnabarina. Flowers yellow, about 1 inch to 1¼ inches across; leaves dark velvet-green, and nearly glabrous above, dull red beneath, excepting the nervures." Its clear yellow flowers and handsomely marbled foliage are characteristics still found — and in some cases very conspicuously — in many of the varieties of the present day, which have been more or less directly derived from it.

Begonia Veitchii (*see* illustration, p. 17) was the next addition, made in 1867, and a most valuable introduction it proved, for practically it is the progenitor of the varieties which give the round flowers now so much admired. This species was discovered by Mr. Pearce, near Cuzco, in Peru, at an elevation of 12,500 feet. It is figured in the *Botanical Magazine*, t. 5663, and described as having "the habit of Saxifraga ciliata, immense flowers of a vivid vermilion-cinnabar-red, that no colourist can produce." B. Veitchii

BEGONIA BOLIVIENSIS. Introduced from Bolivia in 1864. (*See* p. 14.)

was put into commerce in 1869, and is still cultivated in considerable quantities by some growers, its constitution being remarkably good; and this fact, coupled with its freedom of flowering and the bright appearance of its numerous blossoms, renders it valuable as a bedding variety. It is, however, now greatly surpassed in effectiveness in this capacity by numerous varieties, most of which, if not quite all, are largely indebted to it for their best qualities.

Begonia rosæflora (*see* illustration, p. 19) was imported by the Messrs. Veitch from the Andes of Peru, where it was collected at an elevation of 12,000 feet, and it flowered first in the Chelsea Nursery in July, 1867. It has stout red petioles and scapes, broad round leaves with deeply-impressed veins, and bears numerous pale red flowers "like those of the Briar Rose," and about 2 inches in diameter. This species was not much used by the hybridist, but is one of the parents of a few of the earliest raised varieties. It is figured in the *Botanical Magazine*, t. 5680.

Begonia Davisii (*see* illustration, p. 21) was discovered by Messrs. Veitch's collector, Mr. Davis, near Chupe, in Peru, at an elevation of 10,000 feet, and flowered for the first time in the Chelsea Nursery in July, 1876, though it was not put into commerce until 1879. It is figured in the *Botanical Magazine*, t. 6252, and received a First Class Certificate from the Floral Committee on August 2nd of the same year. It is a very dwarf-habited species, with bright scarlet flowers, and smooth and glossy foliage; and it has proved itself remarkably valuable to hybridists, for by the judicious crossing of this species with other strains derived from the Boliviensis and Veitchii types, a number of varieties have been obtained, both single and double-flowered, possessing the characteristics of a remarkably dwarf and compact habit, with moderate-sized but brightly coloured blooms. The inflorescence of B. Davisii being naturally of a more or less erect character, as well as very abundant, these points also are reproduced to a great extent in hybrids obtained from this species as one of the parents; and, in fact, most if not all modern single varieties of the "erect" type, as well as the newly-introduced and exceedingly valuable class of dwarf, upright, double-flowering kinds, owe their best qualities to it. The fine double varieties, B. Davisii hybrida flore pleno, B. Davisii plena superba, B. Davisii lutea plena, Canary Bird, M. Casset, &c., may be cited as admirable examples of the result of intercrossing this species with other varieties; and among the singles may be named Miss Constance Veitch, Mrs. Arthur Potts, and such more modern novelties as Scarlet Gem and Novelty.

Begonia Clarkei was first flowered by Colonel Trevor Clarke at Welton Place, Daventry, in 1867, but he had had the plant for several years previously, having received it from Messrs. E. G. Henderson and Son, as a native of Peru. Though at first sight resembling B. Veitchii, there is a considerable difference between them, B. Clarkei being the least hardy

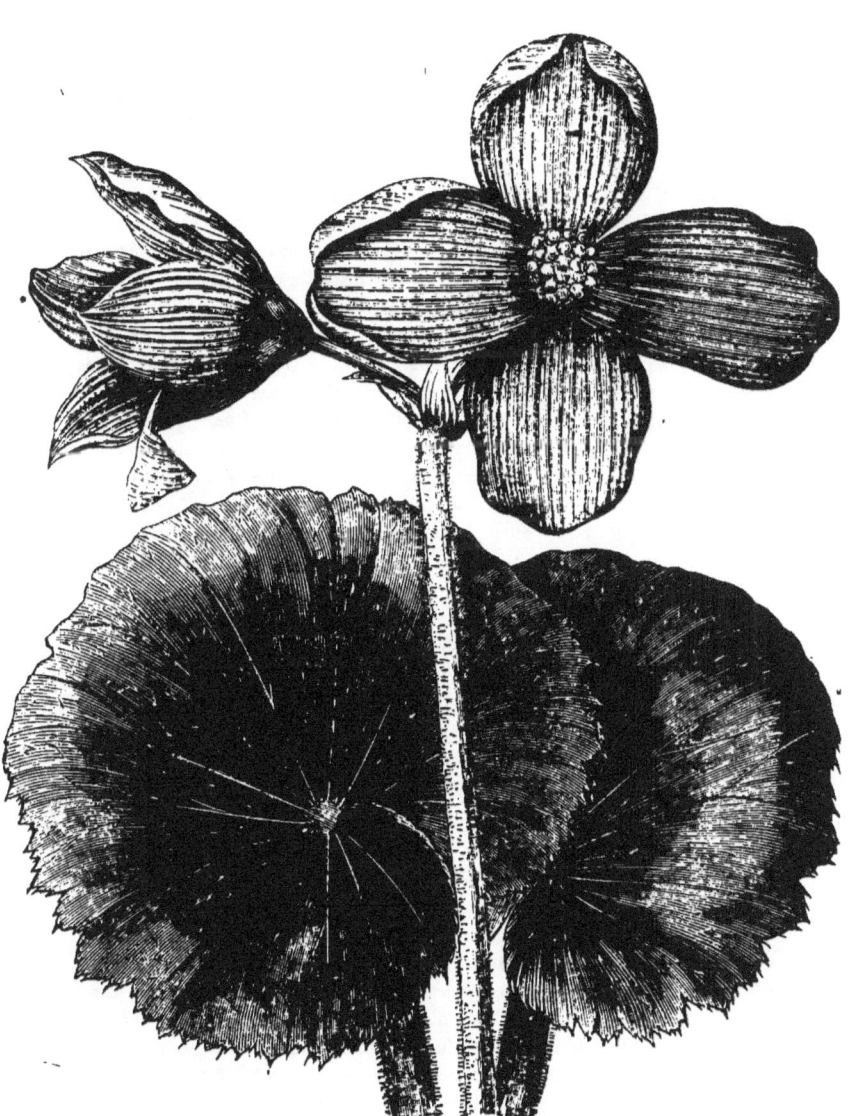

Begonia Veitchii. Introduced in 1867. (*See* p. 14.)

of the two, and requiring a warmer temperature. It grows about 2 feet high, has leaves from 6 inches to 8 inches in diameter, of a dull green colour above; and has flowers from 2 inches to 2½ inches in diameter, of a bright rose-red colour. It is figured in the *Botanical Magazine*, t. 5675, and like B. rosæflora, has only been sparingly used as a parent.

Begonia Frœbelii is another species which should be noticed in this place, and which produces more or less tuberous roots; but as this plant does not appear to be amenable to hybridisation, it must be recorded against it that the present race of Tuberous-rooted Begonias owes nothing whatever to it. B. Frœbelii—one of the many discoveries of the late Mr. B. Roezl—was introduced in 1872 from Ecuador, by the Messrs. Frœbel, nurserymen, of Zurich, and has a remarkably dwarf habit. The leaves and flower stems all rise separately, direct from the tuber; the blooms are small, but of a very bright scarlet or light crimson colour, and very showy; the leaves are usually somewhat triangular in shape, with a handsome velvety surface like that of some Gesneras. B. Frœbelii, as has been stated, does not ally itself with any of the other species, but seeds freely when fertilised with its own pollen. The resultant seedlings are always more or less true to the parent type, some, however, being considerably superior to others in size and colour of the flower, and in other respects. If some mode of crossing this species with the ordinary varieties could be discovered, we should probably obtain an entirely new and distinct race of hybrids. At present it is specially valuable as a winter-flowering plant, coming into bloom after all the ordinary tuberous varieties have gone to rest.

The First Garden Hybrid.

The first hybrid raised in this country, perhaps the first that was ever raised anywhere, and certainly the first put into commerce of which we can find any record, was Begonia Sedeni (*see* illustration, p. 23), sent out by the Messrs. Veitch in 1870. It was raised by their foreman, Mr. John Seden, to whose skill as an hybridist horticulture owes so much, and originated from a cross between B. boliviensis and a species which the Messrs. Veitch then had, but which was never named or sent out. In what year Mr. Seden commenced crossing the Tuberous Begonia we do not know, nor have we any knowledge of the number of hybrids he raised, from which were selected B. Sedeni, and the seventeen other sorts subsequently sent out by the Messrs. Veitch. Suffice it to say here then, that considerable numbers were raised and grown on to the flowering stage, and then rigorously selected, and all but the favoured few destined to be named and propagated, were burnt, "seedling Begonias" being not so valuable then as now.

BEGONIA ROSÆFLORA. First flowered in 1867. (*See* p. 16.)

Begonia Sedeni was first introduced to public notice in June, 1869, when it was awarded the silver Flora Medal of the Royal Horticultural Society, as "the best new plant shown for the first time in bloom." Its pretty rosy crimson flowers it need scarcely be said were greatly admired, and Mr. Seden used his treasure with good effect, both as a seed-bearing and pollen parent. It may be convenient here to place on record an authentic list of the varieties raised by Mr. Seden for his employers, showing the order in which they were raised, their parentage, and the year in which they were sent out.

List of Hybrid Tuberous-rooted Begonias,

Raised by Messrs. James Veitch and Sons.

Order in which they were raised.	Name.	Parentage—Female Parent always Named First.	When put into Commerce.
1	B. Sedeni	B. Boliviensis × species unnamed	1870.
2	,, intermedia	,, Boliviensis × B. Veitchii	1872.
3	,, Chelsoni	,, Boliviensis × B. Sedeni	1872.
4	,, Stella	,, Sedeni × B. Veitchii	1874.
5	,, Vesuvius	,, Clarkei × B. Sedeni	1874.
6	,, Excelsior	,, Chelsoni × B. cinnabarina	1875.
7	,, Model	,, Sedeni × B. Pearcei	1876.
8	,, Acme	,, intermedia × B. Sedeni	1876.
9	,, Monarch	,, Sedeni × B. intermedia	1878.
10	,, Viscountess Doneraile	,, Monarch × B. Sedeni	1877.
11	,, Mrs. Charles Scorer	,, Viscountess Doneraile × B. seedling	1880.
12	,, Emperor	B. Clarkei × B. Chelsoni	1877.
13	,, Kallista	,, Sedeni × B. Stella	1876.
14	,, Queen of Whites	Light-coloured varieties of B. rosæflora	1878.
15	,, Admiration	B. Excelsior × B. Davisii	1881.
16	,, rosea superba	,, rosæflora × B. seedling	1880.
17	,, Miss Constance Veitch	,, Davisii × B. seedling	1880.
18	,, Mrs. Arthur Potts	,, Davisii × B. seedling	1882.

We need, perhaps, scarcely go into particulars respecting the whole of these hybrids, as many of them are not now to be found in trade lists, but a few, for special reasons may be alluded to. B. intermedia (*see* p. 31) bore flowers which closely resembled those of its male parent, but darker in colour. B. Chelsoni, sent out the same year, was a pale orange-scarlet (*see* p. 33). Vesu-

BEGONIA DAVISII. First flowered in 1876. (*See* p. 16.)

vius was the next step in advance, and is still valued as a robust and useful bedder, having bright orange-scarlet flowers. Acme (*see* p. 35), purplish carmine, is still much grown; and Monarch was a brilliant vermilion-scarlet. Viscountess Doneraile, the result of crossing the last-named with B. Sedeni, is destined to play an important part in the future history of the Begonia, it being one of the parents of Begonia John Heal (B. socotrana being the other), a variety raised by Mr. Heal, another of Messrs. Veitch's clever foremen, and which has proved to be the first of an entirely new race of winter-flowering varieties (see p. 74). Emperor (see p. 37), orange-scarlet and a fine bedding variety, was the largest-flowered form raised in the Messrs. Veitch's nursery, and when sent out was considered a magnificent variety, and marked a wonderful stride forward. The next, and certainly one of the most valuable varieties of the series, was Queen of the Whites (see pp. 39, 41), sent out in 1878 at half a guinea each. This some growers consider to be a white form of B. Veitchii, and further, that it should have been called B. Veitchii alba; but be that as it may, its parentage is well known, it having been obtained by intercrossing light-coloured varieties obtained from B. rosæflora, and from it (Queen of the Whites) and White Queen (mentioned below) the present race of white-flowering Begonias has sprung.

HYBRIDS RAISED BY MESSRS. O'BRIEN, BULL, SUTTON, AND OTHERS.

ABOUT 1871, shortly after Begonia Sedeni and some few other varieties had been put into commerce, Mr. James O'Brien (then with Messrs. E. G. Henderson and Son), recognising the usefulness of the new-comers, set to work upon them, and during the first year carefully cross-fertilised a large number of flowers, many of which, being made with shrubby and fine-leaved varieties of the Rex type, failed; but, still, some grand successes were scored. B. vivicans, a fine scarlet, Dr. Masters, a rich crimson, and some half-dozen others, all first-class in their day, were secured. His best hit, however, was in obtaining White Queen, which, with Messrs. Veitch's Queen of Whites, as above stated, laid the foundation for all the pure whites which have since been obtained. White Queen was gained after much perseverance by intercrossing the shrubby white-flowered B. parvifolia and B. Sedeni; and although only six or seven seeds germinated out of the many pods sown, the plants obtained were sufficient to give the pure white break desired.

Mr. O'Brien also tried B. Veitchii crossed with B. parvifolia, with curious results, the plants obtained from the cross having Veitchii tubers with a few hard shrubby stems. The cross, however, proved of no use, as the flowers dropped almost before they were open. Another great break out of this batch was obtained by crossing B. Veitchii with a small-flowered, but very highly-coloured seedling. The progeny was as rich in colour as many of the dark-crimson varieties we have now; but owing to a stubborn habit of growth it was never distributed, but used as a breeder, and produced the large crimson variety, with handsome foliage, sent out under the name of Prince of Wales.

Mr. O'Brien also raised the first two doubles obtained in this country—Princess of Wales and Princess Teck—which were exhibited at South Kensington, and much admired, but which were unfortunately lost during the resting season. He also raised, concurrently with Mr. William Bull, B. carminata,

BEGONIA SEDENI. The First Hybrid raised at Chelsea. (*See* p. 18.)

by intercrossing B. Pearcei and B. Sedeni. Many other good varieties followed, but their raiser ultimately gave up the race after Begonia novelties after doing yeoman's service to the cause.

Shortly after the Messrs. Veitch sent out Begonia Sedeni, Mr. William Bull commenced to hybridise and for several years regularly sent out a batch of novelties. One of his first and best varieties was B. carminata, and by intercrossing this and others, such as Messrs. Veitch's B. intermedia (boliviensis × Veitchii), B. Sedeni and B. Veitchii, he soon had a large quantity of seedlings, from which such sorts as Aurora, Emblem, Lucinda, Seraph, Starlight, and Sunrise were selected and sent out in the spring of 1873. In August of the same year he sent out a dozen and a half more, under the following names, which are recorded here because it is most probable that none of them are now in cultivation :—Anacreon, Brilliant, Cardinal, Caroline, Climax, Corsair, Dazzle, Dragon, Eclipse, Ensign, Gem, Hermine, Lothair, Magnet, Mazeppa, Meteor, Surprise, and Trojan.

Other firms were also early in the field, among them being Messrs. Sutton and Sons and Messrs. James Carter and Co., the first named especially being very successful in introducing new shades of colours. The foundation of their strain was a small white-flowered variety, named Moonshine, and B. Pearcei, which gave them white, cream, flesh-pink, and primrose-coloured flowered varieties, with the dwarf, compact, free-flowering habit of B. Pearcei; and by intercrossing these and later seedlings, the firm has for several years been enabled to offer roots selected to colour, under the general description of the "Reading Beauty" strain.

The Forest Hill Strain.

It was in the year 1875 when Mr. John Laing, of Forest Hill (whose portrait we have the pleasure to introduce into these pages), after some years of patient labour bestowed on the improvement of many of our most important florists' flowers, turned his attention to the Tuberous Begonia, for which he believed there was a grand future as a greenhouse decorative plant. How he has succeeded in the development of the plant to a pitch of excellence at first undreamed of all the world now knows, and we can only express our regret here that we are unable to give more than a general idea of how the marked improvement has been brought about by him. Mr. Laing commenced cross-breeding with B. boliviensis, B. Veitchii, B. Pearcei, and the following varieties :—Vesuvius, Dr. Masters, Mrs. Masters, and Dr. Hooker; but the seedlings obtained in the following year were not of a promising character, but little improvement being visible. He then obtained all the varieties he could get of other raisers, both at home and on the Continent, which he crossed with his own seedlings, and vice versâ; and the next season had the pleasure of raising several sorts which were decided improvements. This little success gave a fresh impetus to the work, and by adding to his stock

JOHN LAING.

the best new varieties sent out by other growers, and saving seeds, carefully fertilised, from the finest sorts, had the results of fifty-seven different crosses to sow in January, 1878; and from these sowings great advances were obtained. In the summer of the same year Mr. Laing exhibited at South Kensington a group of seedlings which fairly startled the floral world, and to which the Royal Horticultural Society awarded its Gold Medal, many of the varieties being also distinguished by the award of First Class Certificates. Then was the Tuberous Begonia characterised as "the coming flower."

In the same year, the Messrs. Veitch sent out their Queen of Whites, which turned out to be a splendid seed or pollen parent. Mr. Laing crossed it with Henderson's White Queen, and *vice versâ*, and in 1879 obtained some 500 seedlings, all of which bore white flowers, and which marked a great improvement on all the white-flowered varieties then in cultivation. They varied greatly in habit, but all bore fine flowers; and a selection of the tallest-growing sorts was named Reine Blanche, while the dwarf-growers were matched, and named Stanstead Bride. The former was certificated the same year, as also was Stanstead Rival, a variety selected out of the same batch, which marked the greatest advance of all, and which was the first variety that had nearly erect flower-stems and round flowers. Other fine seedlings raised the same year were Princess of Wales, Lady Hume Campbell, Exoniensis, and J. S. Law; and some fine dark seedlings, among them being a very small, nearly black variety, of no use for general cultivation, but which was kept for hybridising purposes, and which was one of the progenitors of the splendid dark crimson bedding varieties which were so much admired by all visitors to the Messrs. Laing's nursery last autumn.

In 1879 renewed energy was thrown into the work of cross-fertilising, Mr. Laing having so many improved flowers to work upon, and in the spring of the following year he had 161 different crosses from single and double varieties, Stanstead Rival being the most extensively used variety on account of its stiff habit and erect flower stems. Reine Blanche and Lady Hume Campbell were also extensively used, and from the seeds obtained that season were acquired still further advances in shape, size, substance, and colour—in the latter point especially. The later sorts obtained at Forest Hill have been gained by constantly selecting the largest and finest shaped flowers for crossing, the results therefrom being the grand strain now offered as "Royal Begonias." Mr. Laing has truly done wonders for the Begonia, and in no way can this be better illustrated than by comparing the flowers of the first hybrid, B. Sedeni (*see* p. 23), with one of Mr. Laing's greatest achievements, Queen Victoria (*see* illustration on the opposite page).

The Swanley Collection.

SOME two years after Mr. Laing took the Begonias in hand, Mr. Henry Cannell commenced their cultivation at Swanley, and as showing what pro-

BEGONIA QUEEN VICTORIA. (*See* p. 26.)

gress he has made, we may mention that in 1877 he offered for sale only nine Begonias, including B. octopetala and B. Frœbelii, which, as we have before observed, have taken no part in the production of the magnificent varieties of the present day. Sedeni, Dr. Masters, Stella, and Vivicans were among the tuberous varieties, offered together with B. boliviensis and B. Pearcei. The following year thirty-eight sorts were offered for sale ; but four of them do not belong to the tuberous type as now recognised. The greater number of these were of Continental origin, and few of them now figure in collections containing the more modern improvements. Three doubles were mentioned, namely, Louis Van Houtte, W. E. Gumbleton, and Argus, together with a semi-double, Notaire Beaucarne. In 1879, twelve doubles were described, and ninety-six singles, including six of other species. A good sprinkling of them originated in this country, including White Queen and Queen of Whites ; but still the Continental productions were most prominent in this collection. The doubles numbered twenty-two, and the singles about 100 in the following year, necessitating classification into different colours, of which the variety even then was most wonderful. In 1881, the double varieties numbered twenty-nine, and in the following year forty-two, with a corresponding increase of single-flowered sorts. At least thirty-five of the double forms were of Continental origin, and even at this time they began to show some of the freaks and peculiarities for which they are noted. Some of the flowers mimicked those belonging to other natural orders, and a new section was created for those having serrated margins to the sepals, an indication of a tendency to revert to ordinary foliage leaves.

More progress seems to have been made with the single varieties in this country, and six are specially mentioned as having been raised by the Messrs. Cannell, including three yellow and two buff-coloured varieties, which owe their origin to B. Pearcei as one of the parents. A house of 150 ft. in length was set apart for them at Swanley, in 1881, and what is equally interesting, a number was planted out in the experimental garden there, and which withstood the following winter, flowering well the succeeding year. The double varieties numbered fifty-two in 1883, and were mostly or all, as before, of Continental origin ; in 1884, they numbered sixty-five ; in 1885, forty-four of the older varieties, together with thirty-five new ones, are described, including the beautiful late-flowering Camellia-formed, white Octavie. In 1886, 112 doubles were described, including seventeen new ones, obtained from France and Germany. Last year (1887), 119 doubles were described. An inspection of them shows that they have mostly been derived from B. Veitchii and others of that type, having broad leaves and broad rounded petals ; a few have also been obtained from B. Davisii. During the last year or two, Mr. Cannell has been most successful in raising double varieties, and now possesses a number which mark a great stride onwards. Some dozen or more of these will be offered next season.

Mr. Cannell cannot be described as a raiser of the Begonia in the same sense as Mr. Laing, but he has grown them by tens of thousands, and has rendered horticulture good service by constantly introducing the best of the Continental novelties, and exhibiting them in a condition that few can surpass. Mr. Cannell's portrait, given below, is an easily recognisable likeness of a man who, during the last quarter of a century, has been a power for good

HENRY CANNELL.

in the horticultural world, inasmuch as that, perhaps, no man during the same period has sent out so many grand florists' flowers. During the same period, we must also add that he has, by indomitable pluck and energy, built up a business of considerable magnitude, and that, too, under circumstances which would have deterred many another man from attempting the task.

THE CONTINENTAL SEEDLINGS.

FROM Continental raisers came first the following kinds:—Brillant (Thibaut and Keteleer), bright red; and F. Siesmayer, vermilion; Chas. Raes, deep scarlet; Laurent Descours, carmine-rose; Lælia, purplish red; and Paul Masurel, all from M. Van Houtte, of Ghent. The following three came out about 1876; Madame Hunibelle, salmon-rose; Velours, vermilion; and Exposition de Sceaux. Massange de Louvrex, orange-red, a fine bedder, was introduced about 1877; and in 1878 came Cecile Gente, the first white worth anything, excepting, of course, the Messrs. Veitch's "Queen of Whites." In 1878 came Chas. Baltet, soft vermilion, and Raphael de Smet, from M. Lemoine, of Nancy; and these again were succeeded by Trocadero, vermilion; François de Craen, fine crimson-scarlet; and Paul Quequignon, somewhat similar in colour, all of which were raised by M. Crousse. Almost all of these have now been discarded, being greatly surpassed in every respect by more recent productions, though the three last, Trocadero, François de Craen, and Paul Quequignon, are still to be met with, being certainly very vigorous in habit and possessing large blooms, though wanting in shape.

These were the best varieties extant up to about 1879, and about this time the Continental raisers were somewhat ahead of English growers, the above and many other kinds of less note having been sent out in quick succession by the firms of Crousse, Lemoine, Van Houtte, and others. For some three or four years previously, however, the Frenchmen had been turning their attention to the double-flowering forms, which up to that time were on the whole an insignificant lot, and but little admired or thought of. The first double-flowering Begonia sent out was M. Lemoine's Lemoinei, in 1876, and which was first bloomed in the British Isles, in Mr. W. E. Gumbleton's garden at Belgrove, Queenstown. Shortly afterwards came the same raiser's Gloire de Nancy, the first really fine double, and which is still to be found in the lists. In Messrs. Laing's list for 1877, eleven double varieties are enumerated, and most of them quoted at the high price of fifteen shillings each.

Besides the varieties above named, we had Argus, of a bright orange-red colour; Balsaminæflora plena, orange; Salmonea plena, salmon-rose; Anemonæflora plena, Alba plena, L. Thibaut, Louis Van Houtte, President Burelle, and W. E. Gumbleton. These are now so far surpassed as to be seldom seen, and are hardly worth growing; but by the year 1883, so many fine varieties were being introduced as to be too numerous to mention. Since 1881 or 1882, M. Felix Crousso, of Nancy, has sent out a constant succession of splendid varieties, single and double, every year up to date, and he is now quite at the head of Continental raisers. Mistress Hall, his splendid large double, cream-coloured variety of last year, was admitted to be the finest of the kind ever seen, when it was exhibited by Mr. Gumbleton at the autumn show of the Irish Royal Horticultural Society, held last September; and his fine large single Rubens and Eclaire, grown in the same gentleman's garden, proved to be of greatly superior substance and perfection of cupped form to many of the home-raised novelties. M. Crousse sends out this year five more splendid doubles, of which Lucy Closon is said by a gentleman who saw it last year at Nancy, to be the most magnificent double pure white yet seen; and fine large singles, reported also to be very fine.

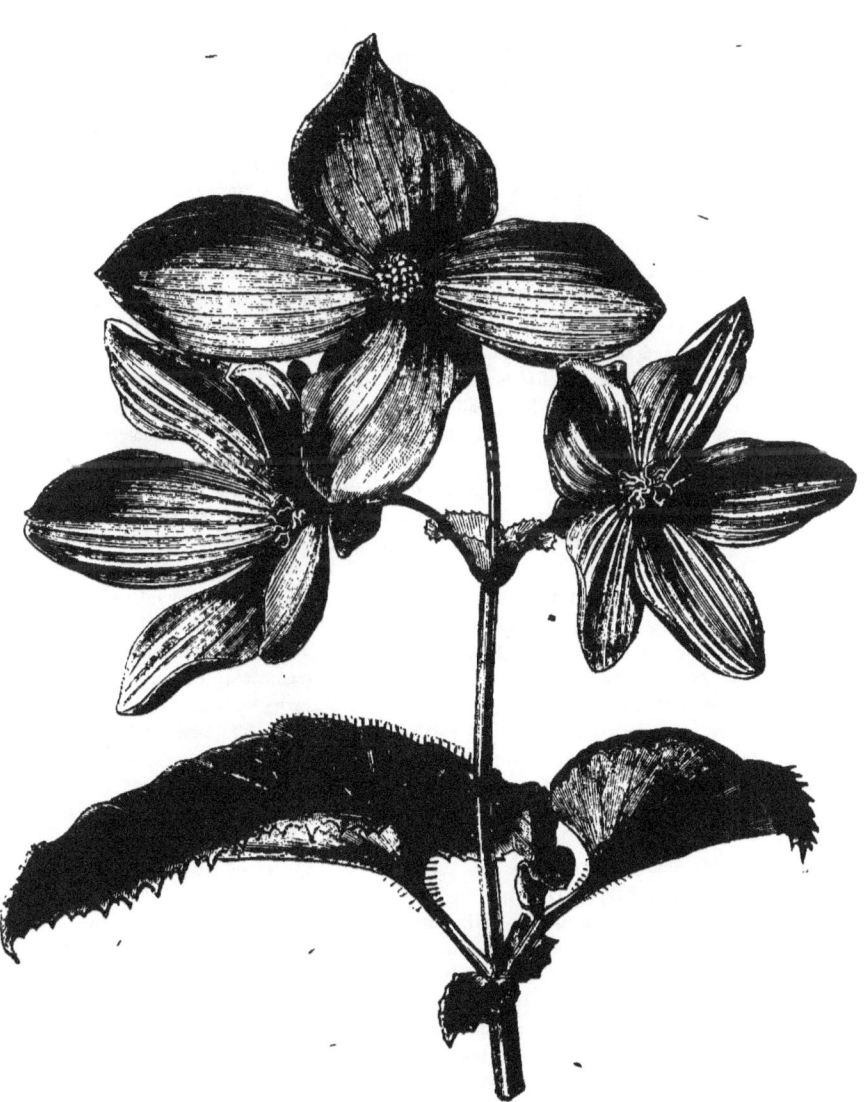

BEGONIA INTERMEDIA. Boliviensis × Veitchii. (*See* p. 20.)

The Introducer of the Tuberous-rooted Begonias.

Before concluding this section, we may be pardoned a slight digression, in order to do honour to the memory of a man, whose name will be held in esteem so long as the Tuberous Begonia exists as a garden plant—we allude to Richard Pearce, to whose energy and daring as a traveller we are indebted for the earliest species, introduced from Bolivia and Peru, and of whom we have the pleasure to give a characteristic portrait as a frontispiece to this book, prepared from a photograph kindly lent us for the purpose by Mr. Harry J. Veitch. Richard Pearce was a native of Plymouth, and was first employed in the nursery of Mr. Pontey, in that town. Leaving Plymouth he entered the service of Messrs. James Veitch and Son, at Mount Radford, Exeter, about the year 1858. Early in 1859 he went out to Chili and Ecuador, and the first consignment of seeds and plants which he sent home was received at Mount Radford on October 15th of the same year. In this and other consignments from Chili, Pearce sent home Libocedrus tetragona, Aganisia microphylla, Prumnopitys (Podocarpus) elegans, Podocarpus nubigena, Eucryphia pinnata, Lapageria alba, several Bomarias, Gymnogramma Pearcei, and other Ferns, Fuchsia triphylla, and Thibaudia acuminata.

Early in 1862 he sent from Cuenca a great number of seeds, Bejaria ledifolia (an evergreen shrub), Lisianthus magnificus (afterwards sent out by Mr. B. S. Williams), Calceolaria ericoides, and several good Tacsonias. In March of the same year, and again in August, he sent home from Guayaquil some six consignments, and among these was the handsome Maranta Veitchii. He next went to Muna, a province in Peru, when he found and sent home, among other good things, Aphelandra nitens, Gymnostachys Pearcei, and Sanchezia nobilis variegata. From Muna he went to Teukaman, where he collected Nierembergia rivularis and N. Veitchii, Begonia boliviensis, Palava flexuosa, Ourisea Pearcei, Mutisia decurrens, and several Peperomias. His next journey was to La Paz, and in November, 1865, he sent home Begonia Pearcei, B. Veitchii, a number of good Hippeastrums, such as pardinum and Leopoldi, the progenitors of the present magnificent race of Amaryllis; and two or three excellent species of Eccremocarpus, which were subsequently lost.

On returning from La Paz, Mr. Pearce left the firm, and went home to Plymouth, where he married, but returning to London again in 1867, he went out to Panama for Mr. William Bull, where he most unfortunately contracted fever, and died a fortnight after his arrival, thus adding another name to the long roll of intrepid men who have lost their lives while endeavouring to enrich our gardens with the beautiful plants of foreign lands. Though a man of small stature, Richard Pearce had a lion's heart, and his early death was a great loss to British horticulture.

BEGONIA CHELSONI. Boliviensis × Sedeni. (*See* p. 20.)

PROPAGATION OF THE BEGONIA.

I.—BY SEEDS.

THE propagation of the Tuberous Begonia is effected in two ways: first, by means of the seed, all new or improved varieties being obtained in this way; and secondly, by cuttings, by which method only can any particularly desirable form be multiplied and kept true to name. In practice, Begonias can only be propagated in anything like large numbers by means of seed, for though there are some exceptions, most of the finest varieties produce cuttings very sparingly. It is at all times a somewhat difficult matter to induce these to root and form tubers, whereby the plant is enabled to continue in existence afterwards, even when in experienced hands; while a single capsule will contain more than a thousand seeds, which, if sound and good, will produce, with care, almost as many plants. We will, therefore, take the method of propagation from seed first.

The seed of the Tuberous Begonia is so excessively fine as to resemble some brown-coloured dust, or snuff, more than anything else; and it seems marvellous that such a tiny germ as each grain contains can be the parent of a huge plant, four feet or so in height, with stems as thick as one's wrist, and blooms six or more inches across. Many of these plants attain such a size in the course of about three years, and under favourable treatment. The seed, which must, it may be premised, be obtained from a trustworthy source—bad or indifferent samples being not worth the trouble of growing—has, therefore, to be sown with the greatest care upon a level surface of the finest sifted soil, or otherwise not one quarter of it will germinate at all. A steady temperature of about 70° is also necessary to induce free and healthy germination, and this should be maintained until the plants become well established and sturdy. This degree of heat is in all cases quite sufficient, and indeed more favourable than anything higher, and as long as the thermometer does not drop more than occasionally below 65°, and other conditions being favourable, a vigorous and healthy growth is almost certain to be maintained. It therefore follows that—particularly when the seed is sown early in the year, as it must be to produce flowering plants, even in the late summer or autumn of the same year—a house, pit or frame kept at the temperature above named is a *sine quâ non*. During June and July, or even in May, as a rule, the seed will germinate well in an ordinary

BEGONIA ACME. Intermedia × Sedeni. (*See* p. 21.)

greenhouse temperature, if covered rather closely by means of a handlight, or a sheet or two of plain glass; but if sown so late, the tubers will still be so small by the advent of winter that they cannot bloom until the following season, which means the loss of nearly a twelvemonth in time. There is another drawback to the practice of late sowing, which is that, strange as it may appear, "damping off," or shanking of the young plants in the seed pan, is from some reason much more destructive at this season than earlier.

The best place in which to raise the seedlings is on a bed of coco-nut fibre refuse in a low, light, and warm house, span-roofed or lean-to, but preferably the former, and placed in an open position. Beneath the coco-nut fibre, which should be laid to the depth of two or three inches on a bottom of slates or galvanised (corrugated) iron, there should be three or four rows of 4-inch hot-water pipes, so as to maintain a steady bottom-heat of 75° or thereabouts. Plain pipes are preferable to a hot-water tank, for the latter often gives off far too much moisture, especially in a low or close structure; while, if the fibre is kept moderately moist, there will be dampness enough, but not too much. The top-heat, or general temperature of the house, should range from 65° to 70°, or never below 60°, or above 75°; and with the warmth of the bed at the figure before indicated—5° to 10° more than the body of the house, nothing better as regards temperature could be desired. In a house of this character, the pots or pans of seedlings can be much more easily and better attended to than in a pit or frame outside, and both warmth and moisture can be regulated more perfectly. The seeds, however, will also germinate very well on a shelf in a stove or warm house, such as an early vinery or cucumber-house, where the convenience above described does not exist.

Preparing the Pans and Sowing the Seeds.

The best receptacles for the seed are the deep round or square earthenware pans made in most potteries, though ordinary flower-pots, or even flat wooden boxes, may be employed when the pans are not easily obtainable. In commencing operations, get ready first a sufficient quantity of crocks, bricks broken small, or fine "ballast," or even clean fresh ashes, with all the dust sifted out, will do for drainage; secondly, a compost composed principally of leaf-soil, old, sweet and flaky, with a little loam, some fresh coco-nut fibre refuse (this is especially useful if the leaf-soil is not thoroughly flaky and porous), a little crushed charcoal, and plenty of coarse-grained sand. Mix this well, but do not sift it; merely pick out large lumps, stones, and sticks. Then sift some good decayed leaf-soil very finely (this can be done much better if the material is dry, and mix with it a sixth of fine clean silver-sand. The rough siftings of this must be put aside, to be used as the best material to put over the drainage. Fill the pans half full of crocks, though if they are shallow a third will be sufficient, or if 5 or 6-inch pots are used, they must be two-thirds filled with drainage. Over the crocks put a layer of the rough siftings, then an inch or so of the coarser compost, and very gently press the surface to an even level. On the top sprinkle not more than a quarter of an inch of the finely-sifted leaf-soil and sand, pressing this also to a perfectly smooth and level surface. Enough soil should be used to bring the final level up to within half an inch of the rim of the pot or pan.

BEGONIA EMPEROR. Clarkei × Chelsoni. (*See* p. 22.)

Now give a very gentle shower with a fine-rosed pot or syringe, and repeat this until the soil is thoroughly moistened; let the surface dry a little, and about half-an-hour afterwards sow the seed evenly and thinly, giving the merest dusting of the fine soil afterwards, just to keep the seed in its place, but not enough to cover it. If the pans have been properly filled, and the soil is in the right condition, every drop of water that falls upon the surface should be immediately absorbed. Now set the pans on the bed, plunging them in the coco-nut fibre refuse nearly up to the rims, and cover them with sheets of glass, and these again with paper to exclude the sun and strong light. These glasses, however, should not be kept on too closely; indeed, it is preferable to tilt them slightly from the first, or to raise them up by some means an inch or two above the pans, so as to allow the air to circulate gently beneath. If they lie too closely, a kind of mould or white fungus often forms on the surface of the soil, and seriously injures the young seedlings when they appear. Wipe the under side of the glasses dry every morning, keep the soil evenly moist, and the temperature regular, shading from hot sun, and in ten days or a fortnight the seedlings will appear, when the paper must at once be removed, except when the sun is shining strongly. Begonia seed is almost always more or less irregular in germinating, however fresh and good it may be; and, indeed, as with most other subjects, the more choice and highly bred the seed is the more shy it is of germinating freely; so do not despair if very few make their appearance at first.

Treatment after Germination.

The main thing to attend to after the seeds have germinated is to keep the soil regularly moist. Beware of its becoming dry just *beneath* the surface, for, strangely enough, if this occurs the seedlings will damp off wholesale. Also keep the tops comparatively dry, or, at least, ensure the foliage being free from moisture during the latter part of the day and at night. Therefore, when water is required, give a thorough soaking with a fine rose sufficient to penetrate the soil to the drainage, or if damp is troublesome, stand the pots or pans in a vessel of water up to an inch below the level of the soil for ten minutes, which will thoroughly moisten it, and leave the tops dry. Gradually remove the sheets of glass until the plants are strong enough to bear full exposure to the atmosphere of the house, and change this occasionally by opening the roof-ventilators a few inches for three or four hours on fine days. The tender seedlings must at all times be lightly shaded from strong sunshine.

When the young plants are showing the first rough leaf (*i.e.*, the first beyond the seed leaves), they must be pricked off singly. This may be performed even earlier than this—almost directly they are up, if damping should set in, as will sometimes happen in spite of the greatest care; and,

BEGONIA QUEEN OF WHITES. Raised from light coloured varieties of B. rosæflora.
(*See* p. 22.)

indeed, it is the opinion of some of the best growers that the sooner the seedlings are pricked off the better they will succeed subsequently. Prepare a sufficient number of other pots or pans in the same way as directed for sowing the seed, but filling them rather fuller, so that the soil shall be nearly up to the rim; water, and let them stand until somewhat drained, then with a very fine pointed dibble make a series of holes in the compost, about half-an-inch apart, and with a notched dibble lift up the seedlings one by one, and transplant them very carefully into their new quarters, subsequently very gently pressing the soil round the roots with the point of the dibble. Be careful that there is not more than an inch in depth of soil in these pans at most, the rest being filled up with crocks and rough siftings; and that while so small the seedlings must not be handled, but be picked up by the notched dibble, and dropped straight into the hole made for them, without being touched by the fingers. This pricking off process is at best a tedious and troublesome affair, but it must be done, and the sooner it is performed the better the young plants seem to succeed. In nurseries where large numbers of these Begonias are grown, several men are employed pricking off seedlings all day long for weeks together, but gardeners and amateurs find it convenient to have a turn at it in the evening, after the rougher work of the day is done, and a great many can be dealt with in this way in the course of two or three hours. Unless the surface is quite moist when the pots or pans are finished, give one gentle shower, just enough to settle the seedlings in the soil, and do not water again until signs of dryness appear. The nearer to the glass the plants are now kept the stronger they will be; admit a little air at the apex of the roof, on all fine days, up to about 4 p.m., and do what watering is required principally in the forenoon, so that the foliage may be dry by nightfall.

Transplanting into Boxes or Trays.

Once the young plants begin to move in the fresh soil, they will grow with great rapidity in a genial atmosphere of 65° to 70°, or even a little less at night will not hurt them, though 65° as a rule will be found the best minimum. As soon as the plants touch each other they should be again transplanted into flat boxes or trays, filled with any light, rich, and rather rough, or at least porous soil, with an inch or more of rough siftings in the bottom for drainage. Take the plants up carefully, with all the roots and a little soil round them, and press the fresh material very gently round each with the fingers. Keep these rather close and warm for a few days, till they commence growing again; then admit air, expose to a moderate amount of sunshine, when not too strong, and gradually inure them to ordinary greenhouse treatment. By the middle of May they should be good sturdy plants, 3 inches or so in height, and fit either to pot off singly, or after being hardened off in cold frames for a fortnight to be planted in the open ground.

PROPAGATION BY SEEDS. 41

BEGONIA QUEEN OF WHITES. Natural size. (*See* p. 22.)

If suitable boxes are not at hand, or only a few plants are grown, it is a good plan when removing them from the store pots or pans to place three or four plants round the sides of large 60-sized pots, which are 3½ or 4 inches in diameter, filling the pots half full of drainage. From these they may be potted off singly, or planted out just as from the boxes.

D

If, however, the seedlings, from want of room, lateness, or any other cause, are not to be planted out, they may be potted off singly into "thumbs," or small 60-sized pots (2½ or 3-inch), from the store pots or pans, or as soon as they have gained sufficient strength. If placed on a board or slate staging, or, better still, a shelf near the glass in a nice growing atmosphere and slightly shaded, they will soon fill these pots. Now shift them into 48's (5-inch pots), or if room is limited, put the best into this size, and the smaller ones into a size smaller, say 4-inches, in which they will soon show for bloom, and make nice little plants and fair-sized tubers, if well attended to and fed with some liquid manure when the pots become filled with roots.

Seedling Begonias may be potted on into larger pots up to about the middle of August, after which it is better to give them no more root-room, but to keep up the vigour by supplies of liquid nourishment. Plants that are potted thus late will continue to bloom nearly up to Christmas, if afforded a gentle heat when the cool autumn days and nights arrive, and more particularly if they have the farther advantage of a light roomy house with not too much moisture about. In case all the plants cannot be potted on, it is possible, and as a rule by no means difficult to a practised eye, to select the best before they come into bloom. A good Begonia may usually be perceived while in quite a small state by the bold, finely-shaped foliage, not much pointed, in the single forms at least, clean stems, and when these appear, wide, circular outlined buds, usually flat and thick. In matters of this kind, however, a little practice is worth more than a lot of directions.

POTTING ON AND SUBSEQUENT TREATMENT.

Any of the small plants that look promising should be potted on at once, and after keeping close for a few days, grow on with plenty of air and slight shade in any light structure. Such plants as these, raised in good time, and potted somewhat firmly in rich, open, loamy soil, with good treatment make grand decorative specimens in 48's and 32's, coming into bloom in June, July, or August, according to the time the seed was sown. Fine plants in 5-inch pots, 18 inches high from the pots, and nearly a foot through, have frequently been had in full bloom by the end of June from seed sown in January, but these were specially grown and pushed on rather rapidly; under ordinary treatment plants will not attain this size until July or August. When in full bloom these pot-plants may of course be labelled and described for future use in the same way as those grown in the open ground.

Towards autumn a very full exposure to the free air will be found to have a marked effect upon the development of large and sound tubers; in fact, if the production of fine tubers is an object, it is strongly to be recommended that the plants be stood out-of-doors altogether, on a bed of ashes or some slates, during August and September, in a sunny spot, and, if possible, somewhat protected from strong winds. This treatment will cause the tubers to become both larger and sounder than those that are grown altogether under glass; but tubers obtained by the planting-out system are undoubtedly superior in every way to any pot-grown roots, starting more strongly and forming finer specimens the following season. Begonias grown in outside beds can always be distinguished by the large size of the roots emanating from the tuber, as well as by a certain rough fleshy appearance, while pot roots are more scaly-looking, darker in colour, and have seldom other than fine fibrous roots.

Should it be inconvenient to have the plants occupying space in the houses before they come into bloom, they may, when potted into 5 or 6-inch sizes, be placed on ashes in a cold pit or frame near the glass with the best results. Here, with plenty of air after the first week or two and slight shade from hot sun, they will make very dwarf and sturdy growth, and if brought indoors when coming into bloom, they will produce an abundance of large and fine flowers for some months.

II.—PROPAGATION BY CUTTINGS.

THIS mode of increase is only resorted to in the case of named varieties, or those possessing some characteristic feature of sufficient importance to render them worth preserving. Cuttings may be taken either in spring, when the young shoots from the tuber are two or three inches long, or in the summer and autumn, making use of the suckers or young growths which are in many cases freely produced from the base of the main stem, or of the stubby side shoots, taken off with a slight "heel," or even of the growing tops of the shoots, these last, however, being very difficult to strike. Undoubtedly the young growths taken off in spring—like Dahlia cuttings—and inserted in well-drained pots of open sandy soil, in gentle heat, precisely as the cuttings of Dahlias are treated, take root and make plants more easily than can be obtained by any other method. But this treatment is very injurious to the old tubers, as unlike Dahlias, they will not produce crop after crop of cuttings, and even the second growth is much weaker than the first, and if more than a few cuttings are taken the vigour of the plant seems to be gone for the season. Any young growths, however, produced from the base of the plants, which may often be obtained from a scrap of root, or the short side-shoots that sometimes spring from the lower part of the main stem, may be taken off when about 3 inches long, at any time during the summer or autumn, and the earlier the better.

Slightly dry the cuttings—not in the sun, but in some warm, moist, shady place, where they will not flag much, but so that the cut will heal and be on the way to callus when inserted. Put them singly into very small thumb-pots, or "thimbles," filled with a mixture of leaf-soil, coco-nut fibre, and a little loam, with an equal quantity of clean coarse or sharp sand. With these small pots, and such open compost, only two or three small bits of crock are necessary. Place the cuttings against the *side* of the pot, not in the middle, only just make the soil firm round them, and put them in a house that is kept rather warm, close, and shady—a propagating house or pit, in fact—either on a gentle bottom heat or on a shelf near the glass. In summer they seem to do better on a bed of slightly moist ashes, coco-nut fibre, or slate, and kept cool and somewhat airy at first, though carefully shaded until the cuttings "stick up," then apply a gentle heat—underneath the bed, if possible—to assist in the formation of roots. Later in the season, when the sun has lost some of its power, a dry shelf or open elevated stage is better, with moderate ventilation, and shade to prevent flagging. When the cuttings show signs of callusing apply a little heat, and encourage growth. In either case when the cuttings are fairly rooted shift each into 3 or 3½-inch pots, using a light mixture of loam, leaf-soil, and sand, with a little fibre, and encourage the production of as large and strong a plant as possible. If inserted late in the season they will not need potting until spring, as the growth will die down before the roots are sufficiently numerous to require more room. Some growers put the cuttings, several together, in larger pots than those we have named; but this plan is not to be recommended, for the mass of soil seems to be too much for them, even when, like Dahlias, they are inserted thickly, and if one goes wrong the rest generally follow suit.

It is naturally a point of considerable importance to harden the cuttings as much as possible before taking them, though in the case of plants in full growth and bloom, which are probably more or less shaded, this cannot easily be done, and the suckers or young shoots from the base are usually more or less soft and watery, so that one can only do the best possible under the circumstances; but whenever practicable, the cuttings should have been previously solidified by exposure to sun and air. The atmosphere of the house in which the plants are grown has a great influence on the state of the tissues; if at all moist, the growth is sure to be soft, and great difficulty will be experienced in getting the cuttings to root, while, if moderately dry, the process will be found much easier.

The points of the shoots are the most difficult to deal with, but even these are very useful in skilful hands; then come stubby side shoots, taken off with a heel, and the young growths produced in spring root more readily still. In all cases the lower leaves must be neatly trimmed off with a sharp knife, leaving only two or three small ones at the top; remove also any flower buds that are visible. If only the base of the cutting can be induced to callus, and emit a few roots before the advent of winter, the lower part of the cutting hardens and forms an incipient tuber. This will retain its vitality if kept preferably in the soil and pot in which it rooted, and somewhat dry in a greenhouse temperature through the winter, and will almost certainly start into growth with the application of gentle heat in spring, and become a good plant the following summer, though no larger than a good-sized pea when it went to rest in the autumn.

Plants raised from cuttings should at all times receive the most generous treatment, for at no time do they possess the vigour of seedlings, and if starved or neglected soon dwindle and become a prey to insects and disease. Still, it is at all times well worth while to take cuttings from any remarkable or really fine variety, seedling or otherwise, and the stronger the constitution of the parent plant, the more vigorous and successful will the young plants undoubtedly be.

Leaf Cuttings.

It is possible to obtain plants by means of leaf cuttings, treated in the same way as Gloxinia leaves, but this is a very uncertain mode of increase, and tubers thus obtained often refuse to grow through possessing no "eye" or "bud," so that, except as an experiment, this method of propagation cannot be recommended.

Begonia Mr. Poë. Camellia type. (*See* p. 58.)

CULTIVATION OF THE BEGONIA IN POTS.

THE dry roots, tubers, or corms as they are indiscriminately termed, should be obtained early in the year, say in January, February, or March at latest (if in a dormant state), so as to enable an early start to be made if desired. One year old tubers, *i.e.*, those raised the previous spring, are as a rule to be preferred, as they have all their life before them; the only exception being where a few large or specimen plants are required, when two or three year old roots will give the best results. These one year old tubers, in good mixture of colour, can now be purchased by the dozen at a cheap rate, and are usually about the size of a small walnut, or say 1 to 1¼ inch in diameter. It must not, of course, be expected that there will be a large proportion of really fine flowers among the cheap kinds, for all the best varieties are selected and marked according to colour, form, and quality in general, when in bloom, and these superior descriptions are sold at considerably enhanced prices. Still, the cheap mixed roots are quite good enough for ordinary bedding purposes, and if obtained from a trustworthy source often turn out very well indeed. But if selected sorts, or uniformity of colour, etc., are desired, then it is necessary either to pay the higher price, or to grow a quantity of plants oneself for one season, and select them when in flower personally; but as a rule, an order entrusted to a first-class grower, who has a reputation to maintain, for a dozen or two of selected seedlings at a fair price will be certain to result in a good assortment. Where a number of plants absolutely uniform in colour are required, resort must of course be had to some named kind of the desired colour, and if this is naturally possessed of sufficient vigour and the plants are carefully grown, a fine result may be looked for with confidence; but if slightly varying shades are not objected to, then it will be best to obtain seedlings selected as nearly as possible of the shade desired. The necessity for perfect uniformity is now, however, rapidly going out of fashion, along with the system of "carpet" and "ribbon" bedding that gave it birth, and on the whole, Begonias are more telling in such positions, or in such arrangements or combinations, so that to know the colour of individual plants within a little is amply sufficient.

Named varieties have, of course, blooms remarkable in some way as regards shape, colour, size, or substance, being selected for superior excellence in one or more of these points; but the growth, except perhaps when in the hands of a very skilful cultivator, or under very favourable conditions, is generally more or less shy and weak, and the plants on the whole not nearly so vigorous and bushy in habit as seedlings.

SELECTING AND STARTING THE TUBERS.

IN selecting tubers, it is well to bear in mind that the largest-sized roots are by no means the best as a rule, that is, of course, all being of the same age. It may at first sight seem somewhat strange, but it is nevertheless an indubitable fact, and one that has been proved over and over again, that the forwardest and strongest plants in a batch of seedling Begonias, which of course form the largest bulbs, are almost invariably characterised by a rank coarse growth, accompanied by blooms of comparatively poor quality, lacking in size or some other important point. In most cases it will be found that the smaller tubers, of a firm and plump appearance, will turn out the best, and these as a rule are to be preferred. It has been found almost invariably the case that the finest varieties are produced among the later-flowering plants. those that expand first (we are speaking of spring-sown seedlings, flowering the same year) being comparatively poor, while as the season advances a larger proportion of first-class flowers appear. Indeed, we may venture to affirm that among any that may not bloom the first year—if from the same class of seed and sown at the same time, of course—will be found a large number of very fine varieties indeed, and no one need hesitate to purchase a lot of "unbloomed" seedlings, if known to be of a really fine strain, and which had been sown in good time.

The time for starting the tubers will depend to a great extent upon the purpose for which the plants are required. If these are wanted to bloom early under glass they must be started in a pretty brisk heat, putting them in about the end of January or some time in February, when, if the house is a light one and the situation open and sunny, they will probably commence to bloom some time in April or May, according to the amount of warmth they receive, and how rapidly they are pushed on. To be had thus early, the tubers should be potted singly in small pots, about twice the diameter (internally) of the tubers (the sizes known as 'small sixties,' 3 in. diameter, being generally suitable), and plunged in a somewhat moist bottom heat of 70° to 75°, such as that afforded by a bed of damp coco-nut fibre refuse over some hot water pipes or a hot tank. The tubers will, however, seldom fail to start in almost any position—on a shelf or stage, whether open or close, where there is sufficient warmth, but will require much more care in watering for a time if standing free all round.

To get plants to bloom in June and onwards, a start made any time in March, or the first week in April, will be time enough, and in this case much less artificial heat will be needed—indeed, a well-heated greenhouse will generally be sufficient. It should be borne in mind that the more naturally these Begonias are allowed to start into growth, the stronger will the subsequent growth and flowering be; but at the same time it is as well to employ a little heat, if only just at first, whatever the season may be, for if left to themselves in cool quarters, some of the tubers are apt to come up straggling long after the others, whereas in a little warmth they will all commence to grow at nearly the same time.

Compost for the First Potting—Watering, etc.

The best compost in which to start the roots is a light porous mixture of nearly equal parts of loam, which should be either fibrous or nodular in texture, coarse-grained (Bedfordshire) sand, and coco-nut fibre or leaf-soil, or preferably an equal quantity of both these ingredients. Peat may be used in default of leaf-soil, but is not desirable; and whatever materials the compost employed may consist of, it is absolutely necessary that it should be light and open in character. With a staple of this nature, through which water will at all times pass freely, and with these small-sized pots, but little drainage is needed, and one or two pieces of crock will generally be sufficient. In potting, a couple of smart raps on the bench will be quite enough to settle the soil; do not press it at all hard with the fingers at this stage, particularly in the case of the single kinds. Unless the soil is in a somewhat moist condition when used, give one gentle watering with a rosed-pot, and after this keep it only moderately damp, inclining to dryness, until the young growth appears well above the soil. At the same time, if the tubers are sound, and there is a gentle warmth beneath them, there will be very little danger of decay, and too dry a soil is almost as bad as too much moisture. The crown of the bulbs should be only just covered with soil.

When fairly up, the principal point is to afford each plant as much light as possible, without which no good results can be expected, so that the nearer they are to the glass the better, particularly during the early part of the season. The root-action must also be carefully watched, and a shift given directly more room is required. It is also necessary to see that the lower portion of the soil in the pots, or the bed itself, does not get very dry, as it is particularly apt to do on a bed with bottom heat. When water at the roots is really required, a thorough soaking should be given, sufficient to penetrate right through the bed, pots and all. This should be done on a fine bright morning.

The Second Potting.

Directly the young roots are commencing to run round the sides of the pots, which can readily be ascertained by turning the plants out, reversing the pots on the hand, all that require it must receive a shift. If started in "thumbs" or small 60's, this shift should be into 48's (5-inch pots), which will be sufficiently large for the present. Very small tubers may even be allowed to bloom in this size the first season, and nice little decorative plants can be produced in 5-inch pots, with the aid of liquid manure. The soil for this shift should be of a slightly heavier nature than that recommended for the small pots, so that a larger proportion of loam will be desirable. Reduce the quantity of coco-nut fibre or omit it altogether, for it contains no nourishment whatever, its only use being to keep the compost open; but if the soil is deficient in porosity, or if leaf-soil is scarce, a small part may still be employed, as we have generally found this substance encourage root-action considerably. On the whole, we should recommend a compost consisting of about three parts of rather rough yellow loam or decayed turf, which should not be of a fine or sandy nature—rather the reverse, two parts of leaf-soil, sweet and flaky, one part of thoroughly-decayed hot-bed manure or half-decayed hops, with half a part each of fresh, granular coco-nut fibre and coarse-grained silver sand—Leighton Buzzard is the best. The compost should by no means be sifted, and, though well mixed, ought not to be turned about more than is really necessary. If the plants are to be grown on quickly, add another part of decayed spent hops, if they can be got, to the above. Anything like fresh or rank manure must be carefully avoided, more particularly while the plants are small or delicate. At one time we were under the impression that the soil could not be made too rich, and made a free use of manure, more or less decayed; but we soon discovered it would not do—the roots could not enter it, and the plants became unhealthy and ceased to grow. Two or three pieces of crock, placed concave side downwards over the drainage-hole will be sufficient, with a few freshly-burnt cinders, a little "ballast" (or burnt clay), a handful of half-decayed hops, or even a little of the rougher parts of the compost over the crocks will ensure perfect drainage. It may be remarked by the way that these same spent hops, when about half decayed, seem to suit Begonias, and, indeed, almost all other soft-wooded plants admirably; and we have sometimes, when short of leaf-soil, used this material as a substitute with very good results. A few handfuls placed in the bottom of the shallow boxes in which Stocks, Asters, Petunias, and many other similar subjects are to be pricked out in the spring not only acts as drainage to a sufficient extent, but is productive of a healthy and vigorous growth in the young plants, and is much superior to moss, coco-nut fibre, or the littery manure often employed for this purpose.

But to return to our text: In re-potting this time press the soil moderately firm with the fingers, just covering the surface of the old ball with the fresh material. The degree of firmness desirable is a matter requiring some discretion; loose potting causes a quick and rapid, but comparatively soft growth, and does not give "lasting" power, so that in the case of plants requiring to be grown on to a large size, and shifted later on, it will be desirable to pot more loosely than if it is desired to bring the plants to a flowering state as soon as possible. If, on the contrary, they are intended to bloom in the pots in which they are now placed, and to continue in flower for some time, we should pot quite firmly—almost hard, in fact, though not too much so; and in this case we should recommend a somewhat more substantial staple, say two or three parts of loam to one of leaf-soil, with very little sand. The plants will be longer in "getting hold" of such material, but when once established in it they will, with the help of an occasional dose of liquid mature, last a long time, and make a sturdier and more branching and floriferous growth than if in a lighter staple. In and near large towns, however, it will be found necessary to employ a fairly light compost in all cases, for the plants being less vigorous are not able to penetrate so heavy a compost as country-grown examples can advantageously occupy. Loose potting and a light rich soil conduce to the production of a comparatively soft and rapid growth, which will not flower with freedom until it has become hardened and solidified. It should also be borne in mind that it is of little use potting on plants that have once fairly reached the flowering stage—it must be done earlier, before the roots have arrived at the "twiggy" condition that accompanies full inflorescence. Therefore, any plants that are to be grown on to large specimens must have a vigorous growth encouraged from the first, and until they occupy the flowering-pots. To ensure this, we must adopt comparatively loose potting, light rich soil, and a moderate amount of warmth—particularly in the early part of the season. A somewhat moist atmosphere, with careful ventilation, will greatly assist in the attainment of what we want; but beware in all cases of a close and stuffy atmosphere, anything of the kind being highly injurious, and whatever growth is made must be properly solidified and strengthened by ample ventilation and abundant light.

A FEW MORE WORDS ABOUT COMPOST.

WHEN the Tuberous Begonias were first introduced, they were almost without exception grown in peat, and it must be said with very poor results. This is still employed by some growers, but we should never recommend its use, except in small quantity, and in default of more suitable and nourishing material. After a time it was found that leaf-soil afforded much better results, both as regards luxuriance of foliage and quality of bloom; and we well remember receiving some plants from one of the best growers, seven or eight years ago, potted in nothing but leaf-soil and sand, and very loosely as well. These threw a few good blooms, and for a time looked well, but then "ran out." Soon it was found that a little loam had a beneficial effect, and the quantity has been gradually increased, until last year we saw that one of our first growers was potting his plants in what was apparently pure loam.

without any admixture whatever. There is not the least doubt that a loamy soil affords more substance to the plants, and develops a dwarfer, sturdier growth than lighter stuff, as well as prolonging the flowering period considerably, although the plants are longer in "getting hold" of, or rooting out thoroughly in such material, and require, perhaps, more careful culture to induce them to do well in it. But once a good Begonia is fairly rooted and established in a firm but porous soil, consisting principally of loam, it developes in a substantial staple of this kind a sturdy and branching habit, and a freedom and fineness of flower, to which plants loosely potted in leaf-soil or peat cannot for a moment compare.

Open Stages—Watering—"Damping," etc.

When fairly in growth, the plants must be removed from the bottom heat, and transferred to a more airy position. As a rule, Begonias for ordinary decorative purposes, for bedding, or the like, do better on an open stage made of laths or boards placed a slight distance apart, so that a current of air, or rather a gentle movement, can take place all round and between the plants. But in the case of those intended to be grown on to a large size, for specimens, etc., a more vigorous though not so firm a growth takes place if they are afforded a position, not on, but slightly elevated above (by means of inverted pots, or the like) a bed of damp spent hops or coco-nut fibre, preferably the former, and of course in a genial temperature. Very forward plants, again, for early flowering, will do better on a high shelf close to the glass than anywhere else, and thus placed we have, over and over again, had plants literally droopping down with fine blooms all round. Watering must of course be most carefully attended to under these conditions. When the plants are advancing into bloom, they appear to prefer a place on an open stage to a solid bed of any kind, the free circulation of air thus afforded not only inducing a very floriferous condition, but causing the blooms to last longer and to a great extent obviating anything in the way of damping off or decaying of the stems, which is sometimes troublesome where moisture hangs about the plants, or in dull or wet weather. During the earlier stages of growth they do not seem to any extent liable to damping, but after they attain a considerable size a single drop of water remaining on stem or leaf during the night, or at any time for more than two or three hours, will often set up decay, which will spread until the entire branch is destroyed. The only way to prevent this occurring is to keep the atmosphere of the house constantly on the move, by means of a gentle warmth in the pipes during dull or wet periods, and also on cool nights, especially towards autumn, when the nights get long and often foggy; at the same time afford abundant ventilation, whenever safe, avoid wetting any part of the plants, and also restrict the amount of atmospheric moisture during the latter part of the day.

On the whole, Begonias prefer a house naturally somewhat dry, to one of a damp nature; any desired amount of moisture can always be supplied artificially, and thus a house built entirely above the ground level, or even slightly raised above it, is to be preferred to a sunken structure. Again, a lofty house suits these plants much better than a low one, particularly during the flowering period.

The Third Potting—Temperature—Ventilation, etc.

DIRECTLY the plants again require it, they must be again re-potted; this time probably into the flowering-pots. Those now in 48's (5-inch pots) will, as a rule, require what is called 24's, which are about 7½ inches in diameter, though any examples which are now very strong had better be allowed only 6-inch pots than run any risk of over-potting. Some of the larger tubers, which were started in about 4-inch sizes, and which are now in 32's, may very likely need No. 16's, or pots 9 or 10 inches across. If the plants have been attended to as directed they should by this time be in a very vigorous and active condition, with stout short-jointed shoots, and abundance of large deep-hued foliage well down on the pot. The roots also should, on turning the plants out of the pots, appear strong, and at this stage not very numerous, but large, with solitary spongioles, furnished with an abundance of long white hairs and a clean, active-looking point, very distinct from the many-branched fibrous roots that occur later on. For this shift use much the same compost as before, but in an even coarser condition, and this should be made quite firm in potting; use the rougher parts of the compost below, and the fine near the surface, and make the upper part firmer than the lower.

Up to this point, and indeed until the plants are pretty well rooted out in the blooming-pots, any flowers that show should be picked off as soon as seen. Should anything prevent the necessary shifting at any stage being done at once, keep the vigour up by a few doses of soot-water or some other stimulant, but the moment the large main roots reach the sides of the pots and commence to run *downwards*, before they branch or run *round* the sides of the pot at all, the plant ought to be removed into a larger size—that is, if it is required to be grown on to a larger size. As growth advances, tie each shoot out to a neat stake, placing these at equal distances, and so as to admit as much air and light as possible to the centre of the plant, and indeed to every leaf. Water, of course, will by this time be needed, and must be given frequently and abundantly, though the supply must be restricted somewhat after each potting has taken place. The temperature should range from 60° to 65° by night, or never below 55° to 70° or thereabout by day. Ventilation must altogether depend upon the state of the weather outside; up to May little but top air will be needed, but this must be abundantly given on bright days; and the blind should be run down whenever the sun becomes so strong as to make scorching probable. This point must be particularly attended to after dull and damp or cold periods, but at the same time inure the plants to as much light and sunshine as they can bear without being injured. When the roots have got well hold of the fresh soil, and are feeling the sides of the pots, the flower-buds will commence to rise freely, and must now be allowed to develop themselves. Feed the plants twice a week with weak soot, or cow or sheep-dung water, or use a solution of sulphate of ammonia (or all these may be given alternately with good results); shade the blooms slightly in the middle of the day, and tie them up, if necessary, to neat stakes, and you will shortly reap the reward of your labours in a blaze of beauty. One other slight point is worth touching upon: some dense-growing plants are apt to get the rising buds caught beneath an obstructive leaf. If this be not released the stalk will shortly snap right off, and a valuable truss be lost, so look through the plants occasionally and prevent any mishap of this sort.

Treatment of the Plants when in Bloom.

A ROCK upon which many otherwise good growers split, is keeping their Begonias, when in bloom, too close and warm; this is a grand mistake, for though Begonias like—indeed, one might almost say revel, in a genial atmosphere, there can be no doubt that anything over 80° does more harm than good, unless, perhaps, accompanied by an unlimited amount of free air, and sufficient shade. As an instance of this we may mention that we have very frequently been through show houses filled with plants of superlative excellence, and fitted with every modern convenience, but kept so close and warm, as to give more the impression of a stove than a greenhouse. The result is certainly a very fine development of the flowers, as far at least as size goes, but the blooms have not the substance they ought to have, and the plants soon "run out" and become exhausted, while a spell of bright or hot weather causes the blooms to "scorch" or wilt round the edges (though heavily shaded), to the great detriment of their appearance. In other places, where the plants are grown cooler, and with abundance of air, not only are they stiffer and more bushy, but both these and the individual blooms last twice the time, and are more abundant, richer in colour, and possess more substance; they seldom or never flag or scald, and require much less shading. Undoubtedly anything of the nature of a confined and heated atmosphere is injurious to Begonias when in bloom. All overheated air must pass away at once and entirely, or the flowers, if not the plants themselves, will suffer. It therefore follows, and the theory is abundantly confirmed by practice, that when in bloom, if at no other time, a lofty structure will suit these Begonias better than a low one, that a tolerably steep-pitched roof is better than a flat one, and that abundant roof-ventilation is a *sine quâ non* in any case.

If there are ventilators at the side of the house so much the better, as they will be found of great benefit on warm nights and still, hot days, when a quiet current of air right through the plants will be found to strengthen them wonderfully. We have often had occasion to turn a batch of plants—usually young seedlings—out-of-doors, placing them on a bed of ashes in a slightly sheltered position. This has generally been towards autumn, and though not protected from the weather, such plants have always—the air being tolerably genial—shortly gained a strength and stiffness, and thrown a mass of stout, large, and richly coloured flowers, such as are seldom seen under glass. Plants so treated always produce firmer and larger tubers than those that are grown inside altogether. In short, everything points to the conclusion that these plants during the later stages of growth, cannot be too fully subjected to an unlimited amount of fresh air. In or near large towns, however, where the air is laden with smoke or dirt, it is not advisable to expose them fully, except perhaps for a short time when the flowering is over; at all other times a slight protection, if only to preserve the purity of the blooms, is desirable. It may be as well to add that the purity of the air, as well as the openness of the situation, has a considerable effect upon these Begonias. With equal care and skill in cultivation, not only will the blooms produced in a favourably situated country-place be larger and finer in every way, but the plants themselves will be dwarfer, stiffer, and more floriferous than those grown in town gardens. Not only has the purity of the atmosphere a great effect, but the clearness and freedom of light, unobstructed by smoke or fogs, is a very important factor in the production of dwarf sturdy plants and finely developed blooms. Begonias are pre-eminently light-loving subjects, in proof of which witness the superiority of the growth and flowers produced during the long days, and in the abundant sunshine of the summer and early autumn months, as compared with that of either very early or very late plants.

After Flowering.—Ripening the Tubers.

AFTER flowering, the plants should be hardened off or ripened by being stood out-of-doors, fully exposed to sun and air, and receiving a sparing supply of water until the foliage has perished, or nearly so, when no more should be given. Any plants that were got into bloom early may, if required to come in again later on, be cut back more or less closely, after having been slightly ripened by exposure; and if, when the wounds are healed, they are taken back into a house or roomy pit, kept rather close for a time, syringed occasionally, and when they have broken again, either re-potted or top-dressed, and grown on subsequently in the usual way, they will bloom again profusely during the autumn, though the blooms must not be expected to be so fine as at first.

All plants in pots that may be standing outside late in autumn should be moved under cover at the first sign of frost, for though, when planted out, Begonias will stand a considerable amount of cold without the tubers being injured, yet this is no criterion for those in pots, which, when once frozen, will generally be afterwards found to have perished.

When they are thoroughly ripened and the tops have died down, the tubers should be carefully shaken out of the soil in which they grew, taking care in rubbing off the surrounding soil not to break the skin of the tuber, if possible, which at this stage is decidedly tender. Ordinary mixed varieties may safely be put, to the number of several hundreds, or even some thousands together, into a box with a little half-dry coco-nut fibre among them; choice named or marked tubers should be placed in separate pots for each variety, with a handful of fibre round them, and the label stuck inside the rim. Some cultivators winter their bulbs in the pots in which they grew, laying them on their sides under a greenhouse stage, or elsewhere; but they are better shaken out, as they can thus be occasionally looked over with ease, removing any that are decayed, and at the same time moistening them slightly, if inclined to become shrivelled, or spreading them out for a time to dry if too much moisture exists. In any and every case, the tubers should be placed where frost is regularly and thoroughly excluded, a temperature ranging from 40° to 50° being most suitable during the resting period.

Dropping of the buds or blossoms is sometimes very troublesome in the culture of these Begonias. This fault is more apt to occur among the yellow-flowered varieties and some whites than in the red-coloured kinds, though some pink and rose-coloured plants (and these often of the finest form and hue) are also subject to it. In some cases this is caused by an unhealthy state of the plants or a want of activity at the root, which may result from careless or mistaken treatment. Sudden chills or changes of atmosphere will also often produce this effect, but in many cases the fault is constitutional and cannot be remedied. Such plants should be thrown away, as they are not worth growing, and no seed should ever be saved from them.

We have found the yellow-flowering Begonias on the whole less vigorous than the others, excepting perhaps a few of the white varieties. They therefore need rather more careful cultivation to do them justice, and they seem to succeed better in a rather higher temperature than the rest, and where any draught or current of air is absent.

DOUBLE-FLOWERING BEGONIAS.

ELEGANT, graceful, and generally valuable for almost any purpose as the single-flowered Begonias undeniably are, they are, as we believe anyone really conversant with them will readily allow, even surpassed in beauty, and in some respects in value, by the double varieties as they now exist. The extraordinary capability of improvement in every point that constitutes a floral gem of the first water, by means of skilful and persevering hybridisation, which is one of the most noteworthy characteristics of the Begonia, is even more marked, and has already been more amply demonstrated in the case of the double kinds than among the singles. Year by year most decided, and in some cases almost incredible advances in size, form, colour, habit and vigour have been, and continue to be accomplished by more than one of our leading horticulturists; and season by season such steady and sure steps towards perfection are made, as to render it entirely impossible to say, or even guess, when, if ever, such a consummation will be attained. Comparatively few persons are yet aware what surpassing beauty many of the newer forms of these charming flowers possess. There are now in the hands of a few of the most skilful growers of Begonias, varieties producing blooms vying with those of the Rose, the Camellia, Hollyhock and Ranunculus in size, colour and beauty, and in form resembling each of these, with the addition of still different arrangements of petals and florets. Indeed, in the course of another year or so we may expect to see blooms the size of a Pæony, and of every shade of colour but blue.

As has been before remarked, the blooms of good double Begonias are of a remarkably enduring character, the same flower often remaining in beauty for a month, or even longer, provided it has been allowed to develop slowly in a comparatively cool and thoroughly airy atmosphere, and well protected from the effects of strong sunshine. But on the whole the double forms do not continue to bloom for so long a period as the singles, except perhaps in the case of a few varieties possessing exceptionally vigorous constitutions, and producing only moderate-sized flowers; this is accounted for by the fact of the large and very double blooms being very exhausting to the plant, and in general three or four successive sets of flowers will be as much as even a strong example can produce: after that, the plant either ceases blooming or throws only a few poor flowers, often only semi-double.

BEGONIA VIRGINALIS. Hollyhock type. (*See* p. 58.)

The Variety of Form.

The blooms of double Begonias vary considerably in form and in the arrangement of the petals. Some have flowers similar in shape to those of a Hollyhock, consisting of an outer row of wide "guard-petals," with a mass of irregularly formed smaller and shorter petals in the centre (*see* p. 65). This is a very fine class, often affording blooms of the largest size, and very double and full. In some varieties, the central mass of petals after a time develops sufficiently to hide the guard-petal, and the bloom then becomes about two-thirds of a ball of thickly crowded petals (*see* p. 63). The colour of this class of flower is generally some shade of red. Scarlet Perfection, Virginale, white, (*see* illustration, p. 57), Lord Randolph, Duchess of Teck, and Clovis are good examples of this class.

Others, again, resemble a Camellia in form and the arrangement of the petals, which are wide and well rounded, and reflex one over the other in almost precisely the style of the old white Camellia (Alba plena). This class has but recently been developed—within the last three or four years only. The blooms are not, as a rule, so large as those of the last-named section, but they are exquisitely beautiful in every way, and are being added to and improved yearly. White, cream, and blush shades appear to be the prevailing colours among this class, though there are now a few of deeper hues. The first of this form, or approaching thereto, were Madame Comesse and Madame de Dumast, introduced from the Continent. These have, however, been put in the shade by Alba magna and others, and particularly by the latest novelty in this section, raised by Mr. Laing, and which has this season been twice certificated—the crimson flowered-Camellia (*see* p. 89).

A few doubles possess blooms similar in form to that of a half-opened Rose, or a Tea, when just in perfection. Queen of Doubles, a rich rosy crimson, is the best example of this class, though several of the hybrids from "Davisi," notably Davisi hybrida fl. pl., Davisi superba, etc., very nearly approach this form. Most of these are of deep colours, shades of scarlet and crimson predominating. Others, again, more nearly resemble a Pæony in shape and size than anything else, and though none are quite so large as a well-grown Pæony, yet a few, when in good condition, come not far short in this respect. Two of the best in this class are Pæoniæflora and Mrs. J. L. Macfarlane, both with enormous blooms when well grown.

The flowers of others, again, very closely imitate those of the Ranunculus, though possessing greater substance, and in some cases being larger. These are exceedingly beautiful, many of the newer hybrids being of the softest and richest shades of orange, salmon, rose, scarlet, and crimson; and as we have now several varieties in this class of a very dwarf compact habit, with the blooms held perfectly erect on stiff foot-stalks, the likeness to what might be termed a glorified Ranunculus becomes very striking. Madame Crousse and Mrs. Frost may be cited as examples of this form.

BEGONIA FELIX CROUSSE. Camellia type. (*See* p. 58.)

Yet another class afford a most striking peculiarity, every bloom consisting of a number of individual florets, each separate and distinct, and on its own foot-stalk. During the earlier stages this is not so noticeable, but as the bloom develops each floret grows in size and distinctness, while the foot-stalks lengthen considerably, and when fully expanded the whole forms not one, but a perfect bunch or cluster of distinct and separate flowers. A perfect example of this type is Mr. Laing's variety, named Glow (*see* p. 61), a very fine bright scarlet, the male flowers of which have become double in a very singular way. The segments of the perianth are comparatively small, and hidden behind the curiously monstrous stamens, which constitute the doubling.

The latter have not merely become petaloid, filling up the centre of the flower, but they have developed branches from their axils, resembling small double flowers in the axils of petaloid bracts, which were originally the anthers. These secondary flowers, or florets as they might be termed, are stalkless, or nearly so when the primary flower commences to expand, and the whole presents the appearance of a dense or compact and very double flower. Expansion goes on, and we have something like a large truss of a double Pelargonium of bright scarlet colour, and measuring over 3 inches in diameter. At this stage the secondary rosettes or florets have stalks about half an inch in length, but as the whole truss gets older, the stalks elongate, until the original flower appears like a raceme of small double flowers.

The Erect-Flowering Section.

Up to quite recently all double-flowering Begonias produced only pendulous blooms; in fact, the habit of nearly all of these was of so drooping a character that they were constantly recommended and grown as basket plants, a purpose for which most of the drooping-habited varieties are eminently suitable. But some five or six years ago, principally, we believe, as a result of crossing the dwarf-habited B. Davisi and some of its hybrids with the doubles then existing, plants of a very compact habit, and bearing medium-sized blooms held nearly or quite erect, began to appear; and these being carefully manipulated by hybridists have received so many improvements and additions that we have now a large number of varieties of this description. And unquestionably the newer and more improved introductions in this class are among the most striking and beautiful of the whole family. Some of the finest of this class, with erect double flowers, are Scarlet Perfection, Madame Dubois, orange-scarlet; Mdlle. Hachette, bright pink; Virginale and Little Gem, white; Suzanna Hachette, rosy pink; Canary Bird and Lady Hulse, bright yellow; and Marquis of Stafford, deep carmine-crimson.

This class we consider to be an even greater gain than the erect-flowering singles, and there cannot be a shadow of a doubt that there is a greater future before them; indeed, this may safely be affirmed of the whole race of double Begonias in their present form, to say nothing of future improvements. Though not so successful out of doors as the singles, under glass we believe they will prove to be even more valuable, from the greater substance and attractiveness of the blooms, as well as their more extended range of form and extraordinary enduring character. The colours of many doubles are now quite as rich as anything to be found among the singles, though we have not yet obtained crimson flowers of so deep a shade; but the lighter shades of blush, cream-pink, and salmon tints are considered by many to be even more delicately beautiful.

BEGONIA GLOW. Double Pelargonium type. (*See* p. 59.)

The plants of double-flowering varieties are, however, as a rule not possessed of so much vigour as the singles, requiring an extreme amount of care, cleanliness, and high cultivation to bring them to perfection; but there is hardly a plant in the whole range of horticulture that will so well repay care and petting as this. The foliage of the double forms is smaller and the stems are finer, almost invariably; but as they are also firmer or more "twiggy" in character, propagation by means of cuttings is rendered much more easy than in the case of the singles.

POTTING AND COMPOST, ETC.

THE tubers are started in exactly the same manner as directed for singles on p. 48, but as the roots of double kinds are finer and more fibrous, the soil should not perhaps be of quite so rough a description, though it must be thoroughly porous, and the plants should be potted somewhat more firmly, especially when growth has fairly commenced. The after culture is also very similar to that required by the single forms, though a slightly higher temperature is advisable during the earlier stages, and early in the season if it can be afforded. But under these or indeed any conditions, the fullest possible supply of light is absolutely necessary, as well as abundant room between and around each plant while growth is being made, to the production of dwarf and well-branched specimens and fine blooms.

As regards the most suitable compost, much the same kind of material as has been recommended for the single varieties when grown for exhibition (*see* p. 67) may be made use of here; but as we have said, it should not be used in quite so rough a state, and must be made somewhat firmer in the pots. Loam of the best possible description, leaf-soil and sand are the principal ingredients, and a compost made up of about three parts of the former to two of the latter, and half a part of sand with a little crushed charcoal and granular coco-nut fibre will be found to suit these plants admirably in all stages, or of any size. Manure, however thoroughly decayed and sweet, we do not recommend, though a very small portion may be used for large plants of a vigorous nature. Peat may be used in default of leaf-soil— indeed, should the loam be at all inclining to a heavy nature, or deficient in porosity or fibre, a third of good fibrous peat in addition to the leaf-soil will be really advantageous. Decayed spent hops, in a sweet and flaky state, we find very beneficial, and if such can be obtained, they may be used in moderate quantity either instead of or in addition to the leaf-soil. Some growers say they can dispense with sand, but unless the loam is of an extraordinarily perfect description we should not like to pot these plants, particularly if small or delicate-rooted, without any, and we have always found the doubles succeed best with a rather liberal allowance of sand. Do not be persuaded to use any strong artificial manures in potting; these are quite unnecessary, in fact, injurious in the early stage, and when extra nourishment is required it can be readily supplied, as necessary, in the form of liquid manure.

A shelf near the glass in a well-heated structure is undoubtedly the best place for plants in the early part of the season, and the reason why Begonias in baskets are usually so successful is probably owing to their being suspended in full light, with abundance of fresh air all around them. Afterwards, when the heat of summer sets in, a place on an open stage, or slightly raised on inverted pots or boards above a cool and moderately damp layer of ashes or shingle, is more suitable and less parching than a shelf. In really hot weather air can scarcely be admitted too freely, a close atmosphere being fatal both to the plants themselves and to the size and endurance of the blooms. At all stages of the growth, however, air should be admitted whenever safe, but in ungenial weather this must be done very cautiously, for a cold draught or sudden chill will often administer a severe check.

DOUBLE-FLOWERING VARIETIES.

BEGONIA ROSAMONDE. Hollyhock type. (*See* p. 58.)

HINTS ON PROPAGATING.

PROPAGATION of double Begonias is, like the single kinds, effected by means of both seeds and cuttings. The former process gives rise to all new varieties, and though tedious, is a safer and better mode of increase than the latter. The seed is to be sown at the same time and in the same manner as that of the single flowers, though as it is of an even finer description, it should be scattered on a still more even, fine, and carefully prepared surface. Good double seed, however, germinates better and more regularly than that from single flowers, and the young plants, though very slender and delicate-looking, are not, we consider, so troublesome in a young state as singles. When fit, prick them off, and grow on in exactly the same manner, and either pot on as required, or plant out of doors in a well-prepared bed to form tubers for next year's work. They must not be over-potted, and unless sown early and grown on very strongly, it will be better to keep them in 3½ or 4-inch pots the first season, though if they are forward and strong they may have 5-inch pots in June or July. When well established in either of these sizes they will bloom more or less freely, but if only two or three flowers appear on those in small pots this will be sufficient to ascertain their character, and they may be labelled and described in a note-book for growing on next year. If the plants are forward enough to occupy 5 or 6-inch pots before autumn, these will, however, bloom well, and make handsome plants.

But these double Begonias hardly ever show their true character the first season from seed or cuttings either; and, as a rule, the flowers will come two or three times the size, or at any rate, very much larger—often more double— and finer in every way the second summer. In this respect they differ considerably from the single form, which, if sown early as directed, and grown along vigorously, make fine plants, bearing grand blooms the same year as sown, though even these, we think, are at their best, and the blooms largest, the second summer. Then it is that a really fine variety comes out in its true colours, the growth being naturally stronger from the tuber than from the seed. Nevertheless, very fine double blooms indeed have been had on young plants from seed sown in the spring, the plants being in 5-inch pots; last autumn, in particular, some of these measured 3 inches, 4 inches, and in one case nearly 5 inches in diameter, though, of course, there were only a few blooms on each plant.

It may here be as well to state, for the benefit of those who are not yet acquainted with these lovely flowers, that only the male (or pollen-bearing) blooms consist of more than the usual number of petals, the female or seed-blossoms being invariably single, and, as in the case of the single kinds, possessing only the usual five petals. Both the flowers and seed-pods of double-flowering varieties are much smaller and more insignificant than those of single-flowering plants, which are in some cases almost as handsome as the male flowers.

The first doubles raised were very pale and sickly in colour, generally of a washed-out pink, or dull red shade, and when a pure white, or what passed for a white at that time, was introduced, it was considered a great stride. For a long time all doubles of this colour were strongly tinted with yellow or pink, and sometimes with green; this is frequently the case even now among seedlings. They were also small and badly shaped. The introduction of Madame de Dumast and a few others gave a great lift, however, to the character of these flowers, and though none of these were really white, yet they afforded a pureness and delicacy of tint, and an elegance of form that was previously wanting, and we have now, probably more or less directly derived from these, large doubles of the purest snowy white, and of the

DOUBLE-FLOWERING VARIETIES.

BEGONIA MONS. TRUFFAUT. Hollyhock type. (*See* p. 58.)

most beautiful form. Blooms of such purity of colour and excellence of form are, however, still comparatively scarce, and first-class double whites are difficult to obtain even from the largest growers, unless ordered in good time, and price be hardly an object. For naturally, the more perfectly double a flower is, the more difficult it is to obtain pollen from it; indeed, it may be fairly stated that no pollen is produced at all by the very finest kinds. This causes the proportion of first-class seedlings to be small, and every florist knows that the more highly bred a plant is, not only is it a more difficult matter to obtain seed from it, but to raise the young plant successfully becomes a much more delicate and uncertain process.

To return a little. After a few years the deeper-coloured varieties began to assume a much greater richness and brilliancy of tint, and the lighter varieties gained a fineness and delicacy before wanting. For several years past we have noticed a decided advance in this respect, each season affording plants with blooms more and more nearly approaching true scarlet, crimson, and other shades. There are now varieties with perfectly double flowers, quite as bright and rich as the dark single kinds.

Doubles with yellow flowers have hitherto been more scarce than those of any other shade, and, in fact, until 1885 there was really no variety of this class possessing any degree of size, form or purity of colour; but during the last year or two we have seen plants and blooms far in advance of anything before produced. For a long time there was but one of this colour in commerce (W. Robinson), but this is now left quite in the shade; and doubtless having once made a start, doubles of this colour will rapidly be improved, and probably before long will attain to as great a degree of excellence as those of other hues. At the same time, these, like the single-flowered yellows, are undeniably somewhat delicate in constitution, and require skilful handling to succeed really well.

BEGONIAS FOR EXHIBITION.

THE directions already given in the preceding chapter are equally applicable here, but care must be taken to perform all operations in connection with plants for show purposes with the utmost degree of bare and particularity, and to have all materials for potting, etc., of the very best quality obtainable. The thorough porosity and sweetness of the compost are, on the whole, the most important points, richness, unless it is combined with the last-named quality, not being so indispensable, for nourishment can always be supplied when requisite by applications of liquid manure of various descriptions. At the same time a soil of a really poor description is not to be recommended, and if the loam to be used is wanting in "heart" it will be advisable to lay it up in the rough for twelve months or more, with a moderate amount of short, fresh stable manure laid in between each layer; the ammonia and other fertilising properties will then thoroughly permeate the soil, and greatly improve its quality. If, when potting, any part of the manure should be found to be not thoroughly decayed it should be rejected; but if the proportion be small, and the stuff has laid a couple of years or so, this will not be necessary. As before remarked, a loam of a fine sandy nature is not so good as one of a granular or slightly adhesive texture, as it is apt to "run together," and perhaps become water-logged.

To three parts of the loam add, for young plants that are to be grown on rapidly, two parts of leaf-soil, sweet and well-rotted, and if the plants are large add one part of very old flaky hot-bed manure, and from half a part to a quarter of a part of clean coarse-grained silver-sand, according to the nature of the loam; if this is somewhat sandy use a smaller proportion, if inclined to be heavy, a larger one. A sprinkling of crushed charcoal, or calcined bones, soot, and "Clay's," "Thomson's," or some other good fertiliser, will render the compost almost perfect. If, however, bushy plants, a floriferous habit, and a long continuance in bloom, are more of an object than vigorous growth and a smaller number of large-sized blooms, it would be as well to slightly reduce the proportion of leaf-soil and manure, and allow fully three parts of loam to two of leaf-soil, decayed hops, or old manure, thereby rendering the staple somewhat heavier, and also to pot the plants somewhat more firmly. In potting, it is a general rule that the larger the plants and the size of pots employed the more firmly must the soil be packed in; that towards the surface should also be made rather firmer than the lower part, and the rougher portion of the compost should be placed below, and the finer above. But, after all, the compost, though a matter of considerable importance, is not everything, and the finest material in the hands of an indifferent grower will by no means ensure success.

Heat, Moisture, and Shading.

The great matter is to induce, by the strictest attention to the daily and even hourly requirements of the plants, down to the smallest details, an uninterrupted and vigorous progress from first to last, both of root and branch. A good grower will attain this object with a soil composed of almost any materials within certain limits, that will afford the right conditions. Encourage a vigorous start by means of a suitable, but not extreme, amount of warmth below as well as above the plants, and by a sweet and fairly moist atmosphere, and at no stage allow the roots to run far in search of fresh nourishment, once they have reached the side of the pot, but afford the requisite supply of fresh material before the plant has had time to feel the want of it, and with abundant light and free but judicious ventilation, success is almost certain. During the earlier stages the syringe may be advantageously, if moderately, used among the plants in bright weather, but when advancing into bloom this must be discontinued, and the tissues hardened and strengthened by a more full and free admission of air.

Shading should also receive particular attention. Hot sunshine occurring suddenly after a dull period in the early part of the season will be almost sure to injure the young and tender shoots, unless they are protected from its influence, and later on its effect on choice blooms will, if unbroken, inevitably be to cause their edges to become scorched and black, if no more, however sturdy the plants themselves may be. But if, as should be the case, a moveable shading exists, care must be taken to remove it directly the sun has sunk so low as no longer to be dangerous. As before stated, an abundant admission of "top" air, by means of the roof ventilation directly the temperature rises, by sun or artificial heat, above a certain safe point, will go far to preserve the blooms, as well as strengthen the plants themselves.

Feeding with Artificial Manures.

Feeding should be commenced in good time, but not before it is required, and this may be taken to be when the roots have fairly commenced to run round the sides of the pot, and before anything like a pot-bound state is reached. Many growers, not of Begonias only, but other plants as well, seem to have an impression that no assistance is needed until a plant is actually starving for want of it—a very erroneous idea. If the vigour is to be kept up throughout, feeding should be commenced almost directly the roots have no longer fresh soil from which to obtain nourishment. A clear infusion of sheep, horse or cow manure will be found to induce a vigorous growth and fine foliage. Soot-water (clear of course) will impart a deep rich colour to the foliage, and ensure a healthy condition. This is best made by placing a small bag of soot, securely tied, in the cistern, or in a tub of water, and stirring it up with a stout stick occasionally.

A solution of nitrate of soda, commencing with a quarter of an ounce, and gradually increasing the strength to half an ounce to the gallon of water, greatly stimulates growth, and adds size to the blooms as well, but this agent must be very carefully used, or more harm than good will result. Sulphate of ammonia, of about the same strength, does not appear to affect the growth or foliage much, but greatly increases the quantity and fineness of the bloom, and is generally employed for "finishing off" almost all kinds of florists' flowers. In the case of Pelargoniums, etc., it has a marvellous effect in inducing an abundant inflorescence, and it is to a great extent by the skilful use of this agent that the magnificent pot plants so abundant in the London flower markets are produced. It has an almost equally good effect on tuberous Begonias, but to secure the best results it should be administered as exactly, carefully, and regularly as powerful medicine to a delicate child.

Where a high degree of excellence is required we would recommend an alternation or rotation of, say, three of the above stimulants, or even of all of them, giving, when the proper stage has been reached, a dose of soot-water one day, with clear water at the next application, next time the sulphate of ammonia, with clear water again, then a decoction of sheep or horse manure, and so on, giving the stimulant at every alternate watering, using it weak at first, and gradually increasing the strength as the plants advance and get accustomed to the dose.

Soft water alone should be used throughout, and this should be as nearly as possible at the same temperature as the house at the time. To this end a tank or cistern large enough to contain a full day's supply, or more, should be provided, and if this be filled up overnight the water will be about right for using the next day, though if it can stand a whole day so much the better. A good plan is to have spouting fixed along the eaves on both sides of the house, discharging into a large cistern inside, so that a supply of rain water at the right temperature may always be at hand.

Hints on Packing for Travelling.

GROWERS of Begonias have one disadvantage to contend with when exhibiting, in the fact that they do not travel at all well, and if they have to be taken any considerable distance the plants often look very different when staged to what they did when they left home. But attention to a few important points will go far to overcome this difficulty, and enable the plants to suffer but little in the course of a moderate journey. First, the single-flowered kinds may, as a rule, be moved much more safely in the afternoon (if not too hot) or evening than earlier in the day, for from sunrise until about noon the blooms are fully expanded, and held comparatively erect, in which state they are of course more easily injured than while they are more or less closed and pendulous, as is always the case during the latter part of the day. In the heat of summer this is very important, and plants removed during the cool of the evening will, supposing them to have been carefully staked and tied, and taken quietly in an easy spring van, stand a journey of some miles with little or no injury, and if they can be staged and remain in a cool moist tent during the night, generally look as fresh and bright as possible again in the morning.

These remarks do not apply to the double varieties with nearly so much force, as they do not pass through the same changes of condition as the singles, and any time when the sun has not much power—either in the early morning or in the cool of the evening—will be suitable for removing them. Varieties bearing large and heavy blooms, whether double or single, naturally suffer the most, and every one of such flowers must be tied up separately by the footstalk to a neat stake, placing a little wadding round to prevent the ties from cutting the stem; if this be not done the weight of the blooms will be sure to bend the stem, and perhaps snap it right off. On the other hand, profusely and small-flowered plants carry best when the principal stems only are secured, leaving the blooms to hang as they will, so that they do not bruise by contact. Erect-flowering plants seem to stand removal better than the others, if the shoots are supported by neat sticks, and care be taken not to allow anything to touch the upturned petals.

When staged, untie all the blooms as far as possible, unless the stalks are so much bent as still to require support, and remove all superfluous stakes, for plants trussed and tied up tight present a most inelegant and unnatural appearance.

BEGONIAS FOR LATE AUTUMN FLOWERING.

ONLY those who possess well-heated greenhouses, with every appliance for affording the most suitable conditions, can have Begonias in bloom in April or May, and they are only obtained so early by a large expenditure of attention and fuel. Fortunately, these plants are so accommodating as to adapt themselves to almost any conditions, and equally good, if not better plants and blooms can be readily produced with a minimum of care and trouble a little later in the season, under much more natural treatment; and, indeed, anyone possessing only an unheated glasshouse may have as fine Begonias during July, August and September, as a millionaire with his acres of glass, miles of piping, and army of gardeners. This capability of being grown, and grown well, by all classes of horticulturists, is one of the strong points of the Begonia, and is of itself sufficient to ensure popularity.

For late summer and autumn flowering—and it may safely be affirmed that at this season plants will prove an even greater success, under simple treatment, than those forced into bloom earlier, owing to the growth having enjoyed the beneficial effects of more full, free, and natural light and air—the tubers will need much less artificial heat to start them into growth, and may, indeed must, where solar heat is the only dependence, be left to break at their own time, without any artificial stimulus. If, however, a little warmth can be applied, if necessary, all that are not above the ground by the end of April, or the early part of May at the latest, should have a gentle heat, which will speedily wake them up, supposing them to be sound and good. An unheated house should, to afford really good results, be on a warm aspect—preferably a lean-to or three-quarter span against a south wall, high and dry, or if a span-roofed structure, it should run east and west, and be situated in an open and sunny position. The heat of the sun must also be husbanded to the utmost, particularly in the early stages, and again in the autumn, by very careful ventilation, and by closing all apertures an hour or two before the sun goes off the house.

The tubers should be potted in precisely the same manner as previously directed (*see* p. 47), about April, but instead of placing them on a damp bottom, a place on a dry front stage, or better still, on a high sunny shelf, will tend to induce as early a start as may be. Maintain the soil in a barely moist condition until growth has fairly commenced, then afford free supplies of water. A moderate use of the syringe among the plants in the early part of the day will assist them greatly, and a light sprinkle again a little before closing the house on warm evenings in June and July will also be beneficial before the plants come into bloom, but after this the plants should seldom be wetted overhead, and any required amount of atmospheric moisture should be supplied by damping the floor, stages, etc. The subsequent treatment, as regards potting, shading, etc., is identical with that indicated in a previous chapter,— but the requisite temperature will at this time of the year be readily maintained without resorting to fire heat, and freer ventilation may be afforded with benefit, remembering only that in all cases it is desirable to keep the house somewhat close for a week or so after re-potting has taken place. Night air, if given only at the apex of the roof, is very beneficial to these Begonias during warm or sultry weather, and induces a sturdiness that cannot be attained in houses shut up closely at night, besides being to a great extent a preventive of damp.

Management in Autumn.

If hot-water pipes or any other heating medium exists, do not hesitate to apply a little warmth during dull, cold or wet weather. Pipes are undoubtedly a very great advantage in many ways, and this will be more than ever evident towards autumn, when the long cool nights, decrease of solar heat, and occasional wet fogs will have a very injurious effect upon plants in an unheated house; but a little heat, carefully applied, will counteract these influences to a great extent, and enable the plants in a well-situated house to continue in good flowering condition until quite late in the year. If the house is, however, not heated in any way, the best must be made of the circumstances, utilising sun-heat to the greatest extent, keeping the house, floors and all surfaces as dry as possible when damp is troublesome; and a slight covering of some kind, if only letting the blind down on cold nights, will be found to make a difference of several degrees.

Shading is a matter calling for a few remarks. Many small houses are not fitted with moveable blinds, and though a handy man can fit one up for a few shillings, yet there are many cases where such a convenience cannot well be had. As a matter of fact, trade growers very seldom go to the expense of blinds, and some of the finest examples of not Begonias only, but many other plants as well, are grown in houses where the only shading ever employed is a little whitewash. Indeed, we have never in any single instance seen moveable shading used in any market nursery, and without doubt these establishments turn out the most perfectly grown and finished pot plants of all kinds that are to be seen anywhere. This whitewash shading, though a very simple and useful expedient, is not nearly so good as a moveable blind, but at the same time is preferable to a permanent shading of calico, tiffany or scrim, for the first shower washes a large proportion of the whitening off the glass, thereby admitting more light to the plants beneath. A little milk, melted size or oil should be mixed with the whitening and water before being applied to the glass, which will prevent it being too easily removed by rain or wind. Putting the mixture on with a brush is the best method, when the stuff should be mixed somewhat thicker than if it be spread with a syringe.

At all times when the sun is not actually shining strongly every ray of clear and unobstructed light that reaches the plants is of importance, and imparts strength and vigour ; so that if the shading can be entirely removed as soon as the actual necessity for it has passed away, so much the better. As soon as the cool autumn weather sets in, and the blooms are no longer able to develop properly, discontinue shading, and ripen the tubers by withholding water to a great extent, and by keeping the atmosphere dry. Under this treatment cold will not affect the plants injuriously to nearly so great an extent. At this season, whatever watering is required should be done early in the morning (10 or 11 a.m.) on bright days only, so that the sun may disperse all superfluous moisture before nightfall. When the tops die down, shake the tubers out of the soil, and store away in some place where frost is excluded.

To sum up, never coddle Begonias ; take as much care and pains with them as you will, but all growth made must be made naturally—robust and strong. Light and air are the great requisites ; they cannot have too much of either. Remember that shading is only of use to preserve the blooms, and to prevent the foliage scorching under glass in hot sunshine. In the open air Begonias revel in a tropical blaze of light and warmth, so shade as little as possible ; and the more air the plants receive the dwarfer and stronger will the growth be, and the greater the size and substance of the flowers. Where the air is pure we should not hesitate in the least to turn a batch of plants in pots, for autumn blooming, straight out of doors, once they were fairly rooting out, standing them on ashes to keep worms at bay. Such plants brought into a light house towards the end of August would bloom grandly during September and October.

THE NEW RACE OF WINTER-FLOWERING BEGONIAS.

AS briefly mentioned at p. 22, a new race of valuable winter-flowering varieties has been obtained in the Messrs. Veitch's Nursery, by crossing Begonia socotrana with some of the best of the modern tuberous-rooted varieties, and though neither B. socotrana nor the seedlings obtained therefrom can, strictly speaking, be called "tuberous," yet this work would be very incomplete without some reference to them.

For Begonia socotrana (of which we give an illustration on p. 75) British horticulture is indebted to Professor Bayley Balfour, of Edinburgh, who introduced it from the island of Socotra in 1880. Its stems are only of annual duration, erect, fleshy, leafy, and usually attains a height of from 6 ins. to 9 ins. During the course of growth scaly bulbils are developed around the base of the main axis, and from these the plant is propagated and grown on. The bulbils should be rested in summer, and re-started in September in heat. It comes into flower in the short dull days of the waning year, and continues in bloom for a long time. The leaves are dark green, peltate, orbicular, concave in the centre with the edges rolled backward, and crenate, while they measure 4 ins. to 7 ins. in diameter. The terminal inflorescence is loosely cymose, bearing bright rose-coloured flowers ranging from 1½ ins. to 2 ins. in diameter. The male perianth consists of four segments and the female of six. The stamens have club-shaped anthers, and are arranged in small dense globular clusters, while the bifid stigmas are horseshoe-shaped and not spirally twisted. One angle of the trigonous ovary is produced into a wing; the ovary is three-celled and the placentas undivided.

CHARACTERISTICS OF THE FIRST CROSSES.

WHEN the winter-flowering habit became established, horticulturists soon perceived that by intercrossing this new species with the summer-flowering tuberous Begonias it was possible that a very important race of winter-flowering kinds would be obtained. The idea was acted upon, and a satisfactory measure of success has resulted therefrom, though it must be acknowledged that the progress made is rather slow. This, however, is not greatly to be wondered at, seeing how different B. socotrana really is from the tuberous Begonias of the New World in its various botanical characteristics. The half-dozen South American species from which the tuberous Begonias have sprung all belong to one section or sub-genus, with the exception of B. boliviensis,

BEGONIA SOCOTRANA.

BEGONIA SOCOTRANA. Introduced in 1880.

the typical or wild form of which differs in the structure and general appearance of its flowers from the rest. B. socotrana is said to belong to the African section, Augustia, from which it differs only in small and unimportant characters, such as the male perianth consisting of four segments, in having shorter filaments, in the six instead of five-lobed female perianth, and in the untwisted arms of the style. These characters, with the exception of the last, show B. socotrana to be closely allied to the pretty fleshy or tuberous-rooted species, B. geranioides, from Natal. The annual character of the stem of B. socotrana and the production of bulbils at its base are, independently of the flowers, sufficiently strong features that militate against the free crossing or interblending of the summer-flowering class with this Old World type. Add to this that the placentas or seed-bearing organs of the former are deeply bifid and often again lobed, while in B. socotrana they are entire, and the anthers are club-shaped, so it may be granted that the difficulties of obtaining hybrids between the two types are by no means a small matter. This may explain the paucity of hybrids or crosses up to the present time; but the fact should not be allowed to damp the ardour of workers in this particular direction, for it must be remembered that B. Sedeni, one of the first hybrids of any importance amongst the South American group, was but a poor production compared with the huge-flowered varieties which now exist. After a few crosses have been made between B. socotrana and the summer-flowering varieties, and these again have been intercrossed with one another, the progeny may become as fertile as the latter.

The First Hybrid Raised—John Heal.

THE first hybrid, and taking all things into consideration, perhaps the most important that has yet been obtained, was raised by Mr. John Heal, one of the foremen in the nursery of Messrs. Veitch and Sons, and very properly bears his name. Mr. Heal is one of the most zealous of hybridists, though, perhaps, at present his labours amongst the Amaryllis or Hippeastrums, and his numerous hybrid greenhouse Rhododendrons, are better known than his silent doings amongst the Begonias. Begonia John Heal is the direct result of crossing B. socotrana (seed parent) with Viscountess Doneraile (pollen parent), itself the result of crossing Monarch with the hybrid B. Sedeni. The variety John Heal may then be tolerably safely said to contain within itself the blood of three distinct botanical types or sections, represented by B. socotrana (section Augustia), B. Sedeni (section Barya), and Monarch (section Huszia). It is very dwarf—almost stemless, in fact—with the foliage crowded together, and almost lying on the surface of the soil in which the plant is grown. The leaves individually are obliquely heart-shaped, slightly lobed and crenated at the margin, of an intense deep green colour, and of great substance. The branches of the inflorescence spread gracefully above the foliage, bearing a profusion of bright rosy carmine

BEGONIA JOHN HEAL. Socotrana × Viscountess Doneraile.

flowers, that hang on the plant till they shrivel. Botanically, one of the most interesting peculiarities about the plant is that it produces male flowers only, as may be seen from the illustration above. The plant was first exhibited on October 13th, 1885, when it was certificated by the Floral Committee of the Royal Horticultural Society.

The Latest Varieties.

The Messrs. Veitch have also two other varieties, which are being propagated for sending out, and which will undoubtedly become popular and lead in time to the production of still finer forms. These are Adonis (which was certificated by the Floral Committee in November, 1887) and Winter Gem, which was first exhibited at the same time. Adonis was obtained by crossing one of the tuberous varieties with the pollen of John Heal, and, like that variety, has the peculiar habit of producing no female blooms. Its flowers are half as large again as those of John Heal, and of a bright rose colour. Winter Gem, which bears crimson-scarlet flowers, was obtained by crossing B. socotrana with the pollen of one of the fine scarlet-flowered tuberous kinds, and more closely resembles its seed parent in its habit of growth and rounder leaves.

These fine subjects commence flowering in October and November, and continue onwards during a great part of the winter. The varieties John Heal and Adonis have the great merit of being easily propagated by cuttings, but Winter Gem has to be increased in the same way as B. socotrana.

BEGONIAS FOR BEDDING, OR PLANTING IN THE OPEN GROUND.

IN many places, where soil and situation are favourable, the tubers may safely remain in the ground during ordinary winters, and will break up naturally and strongly again in spring, but this only applies where the soil is light, dry, and well drained, and the position is comparatively warm and sheltered. In cold or damp soils, or on bleak and ungenial aspects, not only will the roots of these Begonias be liable to injury from severe frosts, but will also be so late in starting into growth as to lose a considerable part of the summer before coming into bloom. In most cases it therefore becomes necessary to take up the tubers annually on the approach of winter, and preserve them under cover until spring, when they may be started into growth under glass, and again planted out.

As in the case of plants for cultivation in pots, so here also we should almost invariably recommend the use of seedlings either in mixture or selected to colour, as may be desired, in preference to named varieties, the only exceptions being a few well-known and proved sorts to be employed where any particular shade of colour or exact uniformity is required. Among those that may at all times be safely depended upon for this purpose are:— Ball of Fire, bright orange-scarlet; Diversifolia, bright rose colour (stands in Devonshire without being lifted); Emperor, orange-scarlet; J. A. Clarke, dark rose, large ; J. W. Ferrand, bright vermilion ; Lady H. Campbell, light pink ; Vesuvius, bright orange, free. All these have capital constitutions, and will not only do well in the open air, even in unfavourable seasons, but will endure being propagated largely from cuttings without deterioration, which is a very important matter.

SMALL *versus* LARGE PLANTS.

IN getting Begonias started into growth, with a view to planting them out-of-doors, there are two different systems or plans of going to work, one being adopted when it is merely desired to have the plants fairly started and in growth by the time they must be put out, which in most cases is about the first week in June, at the same time as the majority of other half-hardy and tender subjects. The other system is to be followed when large plants in full bloom are to be employed, so as to make a display at once. Many amateurs, do not seem satisfied unless there is at least a fair amount of colour on plants at the time they are put out, and in some cases an immediate effect is required; but though, on the one hand, it is very unwise, and a sign of bad management when the beds have to be filled with little half-grown scraps that will not bloom for a month or more after being planted, yet we are strongly of opinion that, at least in the case of Begonias, the other extreme is nearly as bad, and that the practice of putting out large plants in full flower is, in most cases, far from good gardening. A check follows, and a season of comparative rest, at least from flowering, ensues, often causing a partial blank in the succession of bloom just at the time it should be most profuse.

The reason is obvious. Almost all plants that have arrived at the flowering period have practically almost ceased growing, and the pots are filled with fine many-branched roots, while their natural inclination is to continue to bloom as long as possible, and then go to rest. If at this stage they are turned out into an unlimited supply of fresh material, they are compelled, as it were, to begin all over again — fresh roots of a coarser description are produced, growth again commences, and continues until the plants have to some extent filled the surrounding soil with fresh fibres, when bloom is again produced. This is certainly the case with the tuberous Begonia, though some subjects, such as the shrubby Calceolaria, may not suffer much, as this is one of the plants that go on growing and flowering simultaneously and continuously. Pelargoniums, also, of the Zonal class are not injured to any great extent by such treatment; but turn a Fuchsia in full bloom out of its pot into a bed of soil, and see what the result will be. No; the way to obtain a good bed of Begonias is to turn the plants out—properly hardened, of course—while they are in full growth and there are yet few if any buds visible; while the pots should not be crammed with roots, but these comparatively few and large, rather than numerous and fine. Planted out at this stage, they will grow right away, and make large handsome bushes, full of vigour, and bloom strongly and profusely. In any case, they should not be planted later than when the first few flower-buds are rising or expanding.

Starting the Tubers.

Supposing the plants are to be put out in a small state—say when not more than 4 to 6 inches high—out of 3 or 4 inch pots, which will be large enough for tubers the size of a walnut, or less; the roots should be potted towards the end of March, or early in April, using any light open loamy soil (see p. 47). They will probably start into growth some time during April, in an ordinary greenhouse temperature, but should the season be backward, or the young growth not appear by the end of this month, they had better be subjected if possible to a gentle warmth, which will soon move them. Of course they must have very little water for some time, especially if in a low temperature, but once growth has fairly commenced, keep the soil moderately moist, shade only from strong or sudden sunshine, and during May gradually inure the plants to an abundance of air. The last week or two had better be passed in a cold frame, with the lights always more or less drawn off, according to the weather, so that they may feel the change to open ground and air as little as possible. In favourably situated places, or on a warm south aspect, the tubers will usually start readily without any artificial heat, if placed in a cold house or pit, or even in an ordinary box frame, facing south, and in the latter case it will be advisable to stand the pots on boards raised off the ground, so as to catch all the sunshine; they may remain here until planting-out time, with an increased amount of air as the season advances. Any strong or forward plants that appear to require it should be shifted into larger pots, for it is very detrimental to permit anything like starvation in the early stages. But if the plants are to be full grown, or nearly so, and in bloom when bedded out, they must of course be started earlier, say early in March, placing them in heat, and growing and potting them on as directed for decorative plants (p. 48). Harden them off slightly, and put out about the first of June.

Preparing the Beds and Planting.

While the plants are growing, the preparation of the beds must be seen to. Any good garden soil will grow Begonias, if it is fairly well drained and not too heavy or too poor. A sound loamy staple is to be preferred, but this is by no means absolutely necessary. A worn out rubbishy or dusty soil is about the worst, for even clay can be brought into something like condition by liberal dressings of lime, ashes, etc., and by exposure to frost, or by burning; but poor rubbishy stuff must have a large addition of good "fat" stable or farmyard manure and good loam; pond mud is often very useful on this description of soil, as affording the necessary "holding" or retentive properties. In any case the beds or borders must contain a sufficiency of nourishment, but it would be very unwise to work in a lot of fresh rank stable manure just before putting the plants out. If such material is obliged to be used, it should be applied in the autumn, and either be dug in at the time, or early in the spring. Any manure used just previous to planting should be thoroughly decayed and sweet. If the staple is at all heavy or close we would recommend the addition of leaf-soil, half-rotted spent hops, or very old flaky stuff from a worn out hot-bed, with some road drift or scrapings if sand is deficient. Stable manure composed of shavings is to be obtained in some places; this lightens clayey soils admirably, as well as being very sweet. Medium soils can have nothing better than well-rotted stable manure, or hot-bed stuff of the previous year, which usually consists of manure and leaves mixed. Light soils must be dressed with good loam, mud, spit manure, or anything of a rich alluvial nature, as before stated.

Set the plants out in the usual way, with the crown of the bulbs not more than 2 or 3 inches beneath the surface, and press the soil round the ball firmly, leaving the surface somewhat rough. It is perhaps as well, before planting, to slightly break the ball, or at least loosen it round the sides with a pointed piece of stick, especially should the roots be at all matted, but this ought not to be the case. The soil must be kept moderately moist after planting is done, and if hot weather should set in, and the plants are small, watering must be regularly attended to, at least until the roots have penetrated to the damper stratum beneath the surface. In the open air Begonias are never troubled with the damping off that so often occurs under glass, and when necessary a good soaking in the evening of hot days will refresh them wonderfully. Use a rosed pot, and give a heavy shower overhead, leaving everything dripping; when the blooms are half closed, as they are in the evening, it will not hurt them in the least. Like many other subjects, should the weather prove cold or very dry after they are put out, they will probably appear to stand still for a time, but a warm shower or two will give them a start, and the beds will shortly be perhaps not a blaze, but will give a constant succession of bright and beautiful blossoms. When in bloom, seed-pods are produced in great abundance, and as these rob the plants of a large amount of strength, they should, as far as possible, be regularly removed.

The best position for a bed of Begonias is in an open and sunny spot, for, like all succulent-natured subjects, they are a sun-loving race; but they will succeed more or less well in most positions that are not too heavily shaded. A row or two on a warm south border is usually a great success, and on raised positions, such as rockwork, on old stumps, and the like, they do well, provided the soil is fairly good and can be kept moist.

Arrangement of the Plants.

When planted out of doors Tuberous Begonias can scarcely fail to look well, arrange them how you will. A bed of good mixed colours, ordinary seedlings, has usually a very fine effect, but the habit of seedlings varies so much that unless they are selected as to height the previous season, there is danger of great irregularity in this respect. As a rule the orange-scarlet shades, and some of the duller and coarser pink and red-flowering kinds run tall in growth, some of these being very rampant. The richer scarlets, deep reds and crimsons, especially of the newer and more improved classes, are often very robust, but much more compact and branching in habit than the last. Whites vary greatly; some (especially the commoner kinds and those with pink-tinted blooms) are very coarse and long in growth, but a really good pure white will generally possess a dwarf and floriferous habit, while those of the "Alba floribunda" type form perfect little busbes, laden with small white or creamy blossoms. Those with yellow flowers are almost invariably dwarf in habit, particularly where the flowers are pure in colour and fine, and run more to bloom than growth. But these have not on the whole nearly so much vigour as the other colours, and unless planted only on a warm and favourable aspect, or in a favourable season, are not always so successful out of doors as might be desired. Some of the most delicate and beautiful shades of pink are very dwarf and branching; but these, with some yellows, and even whites, have an unpleasant tendency to drop the male blooms directly they expand, and sometimes while in the bud. Careless or injudicious treatment, or an unhealthy state by whatever cause induced—even sudden changes in temperature—is often the cause of this fault, but some seedlings are constitutionally affected in this manner, and if the fault is persistent, it is better to throw the plants away.

The best plan is undoubtedly to purchase bulbs that have been carefully selected and marked, not only as to colour, but as regards height, habit, and even size and character of the flower; or better still, to make the selection yourself. The plants can then be arranged as desired, with a much better prospect of obtaining a good result. When Begonias are planted in mathematical order—in lines, circles, or the like, of distinct colours, in the same way as Pelargoniums, Calceolarias, etc., the effect is not nearly so formal and stiff as is the case with most other subjects, owing to the quaint and graceful habit or style of these plants; in fact they present an appearance more nearly resembling that of the Fuchsia than any other plant, but with more substance and colour. On the whole we scarcely think it is advisable that large beds should be filled with Begonias alone, unless perhaps they be very much varied in height, colour and size, and character of the blooms. An artistically studied, but not too formal combination of these and other subjects usually employed for bedding and sub-tropical gardening will afford a much more pleasing effect, though small circular or fancy beds entirely filled with one, two, or more colours of Begonias, matching or contrasting the shades as carefully as possible, are very desirable and effective. But in these matters individual taste, though not infallible, goes a very long way, and a combination that may be pleasing to one often strongly offends the eye of another, though both may have the artistic taste more or less strongly developed or cultivated.

Suitable Plants for Combinations.

Perhaps a few suggestions for suitable combinations of Begonias with other plants may not be out of place before closing this chapter. First, Begonias and Marguerites (Paris Daisies) almost invariably go well together. We saw some time ago, on a long border facing south, a row of scarlet, crimson, and pink Begonias, with a few whites among them, backed by a close line of the large yellow Marguerite (Etoile d'Or). Behind the Marguerites were shrubs interspersed with tall herbaceous plants, and the rows were here and there broken by Roses, standard and dwarf. There were some low-growing plants in front of the Begonias again, though we do not now remember what these were ; but the general effect, particularly the contrast between the rich red lines of the Begonias and the mass of golden Marguerites, which were most profusely flowered, was simply grand.

Again, a bed of circular or other shape, filled with crimson Begonias, or even with mixed shades of red, or red and pink-flowering varieties, with moderate-sized plants of single-flowered yellow or white Marguerites, placed among the former at intervals, looks remarkably well. The Marguerites, to give the best effect, should be about twice the height of Begonias. The erect starry white or yellow blooms of the Daisies, standing up between the dark drooping blossoms of the Begonias, form an admirable contrast. A bed of dark Begonias, with young seedling plants of Nicotiana affinis dotted about them, forms a contrast, and affords perfume as well as beauty. Strong-growing Pentstemons, too, scarlet, crimson, or purple-flowered, placed here and there among a mass of white or light-coloured Begonias, show up well ; the latter should be young plants, not much exceeding one foot in height, so that there may be no danger of any of them overtopping the Pentstemons.

In fact, various arrangements and contrasts that may be formed by the use of Begonias in combination with other plants are literally endless, but on the whole we do not think these elegant flowers ever show to greater advantage than when associated with fine-foliaged tropical plants, as described on p. 6.

To the above may usefully be added a brief notice of another section of Begonias, which, though not tuberous-rooted, was introduced with special recommendations as bedding plants by Messrs. Sutton and Sons, in July, 1885. By crossing B. semperflorens and B. Schmidti, both fibrous-rooted species, they obtained the pretty whitish pink-flowered variety, named Princess Beatrice, which grows to the height of about 9 inches, has the green leaves and sturdy habit of its first-named parent, flowers most freely, and is readily propagated by division. This has since proved to be an admirable bedding plant. By crossing a shrubby variety, with green leaves, spotted with white, selected from some seedlings obtained from B. Rex, with the pollen of a light scarlet tuberous-rooted variety—a seedling from B. Davisii—Messrs. Sutton and Sons obtained about the same time a variety which they named Prince Henry, and which was certificated by the Floral Committee on account of its dwarf compact habit, and the freedom with which it produced its small bright red blossoms. It had all the merits of a good bedding plant, but has, we believe, been lost to cultivation.

Preserving the Tubers in Winter.

When the flowering is over, and the tops have been touched by the first slight frost, take the tubers up, having previously labelled and marked them as to colour, height, etc., as a guide for the following season, and store them away in pots or boxes, with a little half-dry coco-nut fibre around the tubers. (*See* also p. 55.)

Should it be considered safe to leave them in the ground, each plant or row of plants should, especially if the tubers are near the surface, be covered with a heap of ashes, coco-nut fibre refuse, or moss, to a depth of six or eight inches, which will exclude a considerable degree of frost. If, however, the ground is likely to require fresh nourishment, it would be better to lay on a few inches of short, partly-decayed manure, in a somewhat dry and flaky condition, and over this some dry bracken or litter. This last can be removed early in spring, and the manure then carefully forked in between the plants, will be found to benefit them considerably.

SEED SAVING AND HYBRIDISATION.

WHEN the principles of cultivation are thoroughly mastered, down to the minutest details, and the conditions necessary to ensure success are rightly understood—not before—the ambitious and persevering grower, be it of Begonias or any other subject, may enter the more scientific and wider field of hybridisation; and supposing him to be possessed of the true florist's spirit, he will find the occupation of crossing the different varieties, and raising seedlings from the resultant germs, a most fascinating as well as an instructive and profitable amusement. But until the secret of growing the plants to perfection, or nearly so, has been learnt—until, in fact, the alphabet of floriculture has been mastered, it is useless to attempt the more ambitious task—as useless and inconsequential as it would be for a child to attempt to read before learning its letters, or for a tyro to try to perform on an instrument before he has mastered the notes and scales.

This much may be safely and most positively stated, that no flower we possess will so surely and certainly—and, indeed, so quickly also—repay the hybridist for any amount of care, thought and trouble that may be bestowed on it, as the Tuberous Begonia. The process of fertilisation and seed saving is really, like many other things, by no means difficult or intricate when you know how to do it. And once the principles have been grasped, nothing can be more fascinating and pleasing than, season after season, to watch the successional expanding of the results of the previous year's labours, and note the gradual but certain steps towards perfection that are gained, which in their turn become the starting point for fresh endeavours and successes.

THE PROPERTIES OF A SINGLE BEGONIA.

BEFORE proceeding farther, it may be as well to state the points of good Begonias, or those qualities which it is the constant aim of growers to produce in the highest degree.

Form is undoubtedly the most important. The circular form, with broad overlapping petals, developed to the highest possible point, is the standard of perfection here, as in the case of the Zonal Pelargonium. The earliest varieties had flowers composed of long narrow petals, forming what is termed

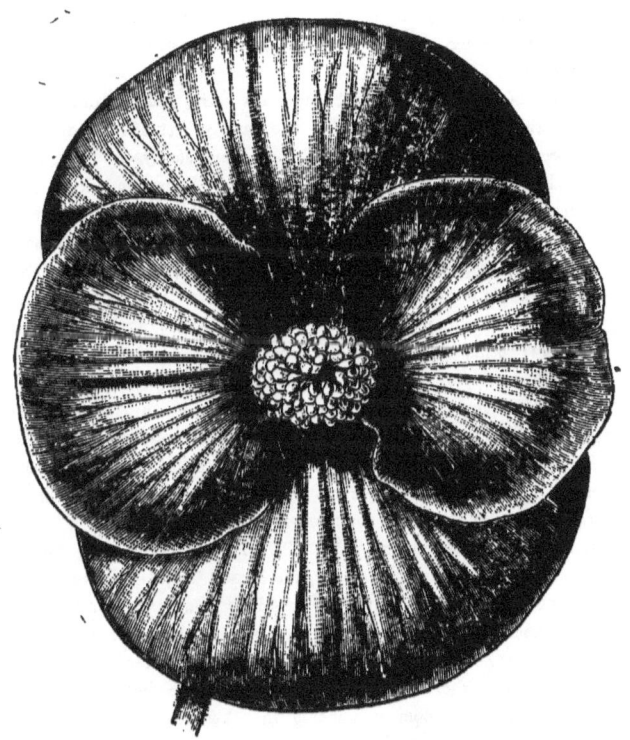

BEGONIA ROSE CÉLESTE. Improved form. (*See* p. 88.)

a loose bloom, that is, with spaces between each petal when the flower was fully expanded. By degrees something better, as will be seen by reference to the illustrations of the hybrids which succeeded B. Sedeni, was produced, while the illustrations of Mr. Laing and Mr. Cannell's modern flowers in previous pages give a pretty correct idea of the form of the finest circular blooms of the present day. The roundness, regularity and finish of the petals, and, indeed, of the whole bloom, each and all count for a great deal; and it is also necessary that a good flower should open well, that is to say, that the petals should lie flat, or nearly so, when the bloom is fully expanded. Some varieties assume a slightly cup-shaped form, and this is sometimes both graceful and effective ; but a perfect bloom is as nearly flat as possible, while anything more than a very slight reflex is quite inadmissible. If the petals curl or twist in opening at all, the flower is quite spoiled, however fine in ther respects

Colour may be taken as the next important point, and the clearer, richer, and brighter this is, the more valuable the variety becomes. Years ago the colours of Begonias were, as a rule, dull, pale, and sickly—at least, as compared with what we have now ; and when the variety known as "J. H. Laing" was produced, it was considered a grand stride, and for some time was the brightest scarlet or light crimson in cultivation. This has now been long surpassed, and we have plenty of varieties as rich and bright in colour as the finest Zonal Pelargoniums, while in a few instances there is a depth and velvety softness, or dazzling intensity of hue that is very striking, and hardly equalled by any other flower, except, perhaps, the Gloxinia. Whites and yellows as well should, of course, be as pure in tone as possible.

Substance is a very important characteristic, a poor, thin or flimsy flower being next to worthless, however large or fine in other respects. Some of the newer varieties have petals almost like a bit of leather, when felt between the fingers—a great advance on the old flimsy-textured blooms, which would hardly bear looking at, to use a common expression.

Size may be taken as coming next. This is constantly being increased ; twenty years ago, or even less than that, the largest Begonia flowers measured only about one inch across, about 1880 a 4-inch flower was considered very large indeed, and now we have plenty that will reach 6 inches from top to bottom, and some 7 inches and even 8 inches in diameter. What a wonderful alteration in so short a space of time ! Mere size, however, should not count for much, if the bloom is wanting in other respects. The medium sized blooms, such as the one illustrated on p. 87, are, to our thinking, quite large enough, and this view is shared to a large extent by Mr. Laing.

Freedom of flowering counts considerably, and it is, of course, to be seen at a glance whether a plant is a shy bloomer or tho reverse. It is not to be expected that any plant will produce flowers of the largest size as freely as one with comparatively small blooms, but it is as well to have the two qualities combined as far as possible.

Habit of growth is another important point. In this respect most of the varieties raised on the Continent are decidedly deficient, often running up to a considerable height with only one or two main stems—in fact, what in generally known as "leggy." English-raised seedlings are generally much superior in this respect, and seedling plants are almost invariably more bushy in growth than propagated named varieties. A medium-sized flowering plant should branch naturally and freely, so as to form a many-shooted bush,

BEGONIA CAMELLIA. Example of a good type. (*See* p. 90.)

covered with an abundance of blossoms; but very large-flowered kinds do not, as a rule, and indeed should not ramify so much, and three or four main stems on a moderate-sized plant is quite sufficient, for if the growth is much divided the blooms will of course suffer in size. Yet in all cases the growth should be stout and compact, with strong and healthy foliage right down to the pot. The size of the individual trusses makes a great difference in the

G

appearance of a plant—of course if these are very abundantly produced they need not, and indeed cannot be of very great size; but some of the finest new varieties (single), throw such a mass of blooms of the largest size on a single stem, that even three or four on a plant affords a grand appearance. Begonias, the single kinds more particularly, almost invariably bloom in threes, of which the centre is always a male flower, and the two side ones generally female, though frequently one, and sometimes both these are male also. The old-fashioned kinds, as a rule, only produced one of these triplets on a footstalk, whereas the strong-growing hybrids of the present day will often throw *three* sets of three blooms, making nine, or occasionally even more flowers on a single stalk, and these will be sometimes all expanded at the same time.

Hardiness and vigour of constitution are points of great importance, particularly in kinds intended for bedding-out purposes, but unless the growth of a plant is evidently weak or sickly, it is plain that no determination could be come to on this point from a single inspection, as in judging at shows, etc. It is the form, size, colour, and substance of the individual blooms, and the habit and floriferousness of the plant that go to make a fine specimen and a good show on the exhibition table, no matter by what means the result may be obtained.

The Points of a Double Begonia.

The points of a first-class Double Begonia are more difficult to define. Size is of course desirable up to a certain point, though a well-shaped, medium-sized bloom is, in our opinion, much to be preferred to a huge unshapely mass of petals. Camellia, the variety illustrated on p. 89, is quite large enough. Colour naturally counts largely, and the more rich, or dense, and pure this is, the more valuable does the plant become. Form is a very important point, but this varies so greatly that it is impossible to set up a standard, or lay down any hard and fast rule. Round or circular-outlined petals, well arranged and of good colour, are in most cases to be preferred, but some varieties with narrow-pointed petals are very handsome. The most objectionable kinds are, in our opinion, those that consist of an irregular mass of crinkled petals, and yet if these in any way approach the Hollyhock form they become beautiful directly. Substance of petal is of great importance, and affords a lasting quality to the whole bloom. A good habit and freedom in flowering of the plant itself are naturally very desirable in this as in the single Begonia.

How and when to Manipulate the Blooms.

Having now indicated, as nearly as may be, the object to be attained, let us proceed to operations. The first necessity is of course a good number—and

SEED SAVING AND HYBRIDISATION.

the more and the greater variety among them the better—of plants of the highest excellence, with a suitable structure in which to flower them and manipulate the blooms. This, as has been already directed in the chapters on general culture, should be a light, roomy, and well-ventilated house, properly heated, and, if possible, span-roofed, and situated in an open and sunny spot. It should also be of a naturally dry nature, or capable of being at any time allowed to become so, for neither can fertilisation be so successfully performed, nor will the seed-containing pods so surely and perfectly set and ripen, if there is any amount of latent dampness, as when the atmosphere is fairly and reasonably dry. This becomes a very important factor in obtaining a successful result with late-saved seed, which cannot be ripened at all except in a dry and warm structure. All Begonia houses should therefore be built entirely above ground, and well drained from any possible lodgment of water in or near them.

The seed-pods may be "set," as it is termed, at any time that the plants are in bloom, or from the month of May until the end of October, or nearly so; but there are reasons why the operation should not, if it can be avoided, be performed either very early or very late in the season. In the first place, it is bad policy to commence fertilising while the plants are still not much advanced, particularly where a long succession of bloom is expected, for nothing exhausts the plants more quickly or shortens the period of flowering than the formation of seed-pods. Again, it is unwise either to defer the operation until so late that the plants are past their best, and the blooms and resultant seed-pods comparatively small and weak, when the seed will be neither so plentiful nor so good as if it were saved at an earlier stage; or to leave it until the advent of the cold, damp, and often sunless days of late autumn, which under ordinary circumstances will seriously interfere with both successful fertilisation and the subsequent ripening of the pods and seed. In high, warm, and dry situations it is, of course, quite possible to save and ripen seed much later than in less favoured localities; we have seen splendid pods set in October, and even later, and gathered in good condition near Christmas.

A dry house, properly heated, and in a warm and favourable position, is a great advantage to the hybridist, as it often enables him to obtain seed from those plants, among the seedlings of the same year that do not arrive at a flowering state until late in the season; and among these are found, as has been already remarked, some of the finest varieties of the whole batch. In other words, the cultivator can thus work on the *current* year's stock, which should be an advance upon that of the previous season, and thus a gain of about a twelvemonth is practically effected. It may be remarked here, that we do not consider it by any means advisable to obtain anything like a heavy crop of seed from young plants raised the same year—one or two pods only should be allowed to set and ripen, or the result of the strain upon the immature plant may be painfully apparent next season. Also, when it is desired to save seed from plants in the early stage of flowering, and particularly where a specially choice sample of seed is required, it will also be well to set only one, two, or at most three pods on a single plant, and the last number only on a very strong example.

Where a dry heat cannot be applied, or, indeed, under unfavourable conditions of any kind, it is advisable to get the blooms fertilised and the pods "set," as far as possible, during the month of July or early in August, when they will take freely, ripen without trouble, and probably be fit to harvest some time in August or September. At the time of fertilising the blooms, and while the pods are swelling and ripening, it is advisable to keep the atmosphere of the house as dry (in reason) as will agree with the health of the other inmates, particularly should the prevailing weather be cold and damp; and, also, to be rather more sparing in the supply of water at the root than usual. A gentle warmth in the pipes is also of great use, drying the air and promoting evaporation and a healthy movement in the atmosphere; and an open stage is often more suitable than a close one.

Natural Fertilisation.

BEGONIAS, both single and double, but more frequently the former, will often set and mature seed-pods without any artificial fertilisation whatever, though it is probable that this takes place unnoticed by the pollen being carried in the air, or in some cases by insects, from one flower to another. But this naturally fertilised seed, or such as has been inoculated by chance, is comparatively worthless, or, at any rate, cannot be depended upon, even though the parent blooms were of good quality. At the same time, it is quite possible for a really good cross to be effected in this hap-hazard fashion, and it occasionally happens that very valuable seedlings are obtained by chance in this way. In appears to be an invariable rule that commoner varieties or indifferent flowers are fertilised and produce seed much more readily than those that are more highly bred; and the finer the flowers are, the more shy do they become of seed-bearing. Indeed, in a large collection of the very finest varieties we have known scarcely a single seed-pod to be produced except those that had been carefully fertilised by hand. But undoubtedly thorough artificial inoculation is the only true scientific and certain mode of effecting the desired object, and in this way only should the cultivator attempt to obtain seed.

Artificial Fertilisation.

THE *modus operandi* is not always identical, some growers preferring to employ a camel-hair brush to effect the transfer of pollen; and where great exactness is not required, as in the production of ordinary good mixed seed in quantity, it is usual to work indiscriminately by this means among any blooms of good quality. But where exact and distinct crosses are to be made, the best method is to apply the mass of pollen-bearing anthers of the male bloom directly to the stigma of the female, which in the Begonia consists of three pairs of corkscrew-shaped processes. In order to accomplish this, the male flower must, of course, either be plucked, or the two plants brought so close together that the blooms can be brought into contact while still attached; or we have often employed male blooms that have recently fallen from the plants, when they will often be found to retain a considerable amount of pollen. By this means the entirety of the stigma, or stigmas, are thoroughly covered with pollen, and all the cells of the pod are impregnated and become filled with fertile seed. This operation should always (whenever possible) be performed while the sun is shining, and in the middle of the day if practicable, or at any rate between the limits of ten o'clock in the forenoon and three or four o'clock p.m. We do not say that the pollen will not "take" to a greater or less extent when actual sunshine is not present, for, unlike some other plants, such as the Pelargonium and Petunia, not a pod or seed of which will "set" upon a dull day, however carefully impregnated, the Begonia is by no means shy of seeding, but the operation is much more surely and effectually accomplished under the immediate supervision of "old Sol," and we should further recommend any particularly choice crosses to be made between the hours of ten and twelve a.m.

It should, moreover, be borne in mind that the choicest and most highly bred varieties are almost invariably shy of seeding, and must be operated on under the most favorable conditions all round to ensure success; common kinds produce seed abundantly with little or no trouble. It occasionally happens that particular blooms are fit for fertilisation at unpropitious times, as regards the weather, etc.; in such cases the best that is possible must be done under the circumstances, remembering that a dry atmosphere, a moderately dry condition of the soil in the pots, and if cold or damp prevails, a gentle heat in the pipes will greatly conduce to success. Pollen may even be kept a few days in extreme cases, placing it in a piece of clean folded paper, but it is better used fresh whenever possible.

Marking the Crosses—Gathering the Seeds.

The operation performed, the different crosses may be distinguished by means of short pieces of coloured cotton, silk, etc., tied round the footstalk of the bloom, and the particulars entered in a note-book. The most favourable stage for the blooms to be operated upon is, in the case of the female or seed-bearing flower, directly it is thoroughly expanded, say about the third day after it first opens, and before it can have become inoculated by insects or any flying pollen; and in the case of the male flower as soon as the pollen falls freely. Should bees or other insects prove troublesome, and likely to disturb your arrangements, exclude them from the house by nailing fine wire netting, or some kind of perforated material over the ventilators ; or the house, if a roomy one, and the weather is not too hot, may be kept closed for two or three days. Some have even recommended enclosing the blooms (which can be stripped of their petals without injury) in little bags of muslin or oiled silk, but we have never found it necessary to be so particular as this, as thorough impregnation at the right time seldom fails.

If the "cross" has "taken" properly, the fact will be made known by the falling of the petals within forty-eight hours at the farthest—usually within twenty-four hours—from the time the operation was performed. When the pods are properly set and are swelling up, they should be kept perfectly dry, freely subjected to the influence of light and air, and a fair amount of sun acting upon them will also be found beneficial. When they turn brown, but before they burst, gather and lay them on pieces of clean paper in some sunny, protected place, and when thoroughly ripe, shake out the seed and place it in strong paper pockets.

Selecting the Flowers for Crossing.

The method of fertilisation having now, we trust, been made pretty clear, let us proceed to consider the rules that govern the important point of selection. In the first place it may be taken as an axiom, that if an improvement in the quality of the flowers is desired, this can only be brought about by cross-fertilisation (breeding). Inoculating the female blooms of a plant with pollen from its own male blooms, causes a stricter adherence to the characteristics of the parent, but it is very seldom that any real improvement is effected by this course of procedure. Indeed, it may be fairly said that in this respect plants resemble animals, for what is known as inbreeding, especially when this is continued for several generations, is in both undoubtedly injurious to the qualities of the race or "strain"; whereas the constant inter-crossing of individuals differing widely in one or more points from each other, or, in other words, the repeated introduction of fresh "blood," is almost always productive of a class possessing remarkable vigour, and superior in many points to the parent stock. Careful selection has, of course, a great deal to do with success.

Reducing this to practice, it will be found that the inter-crossing of plants or blooms possessing widely different qualities (though each must have really good points), will be unfailingly productive of great improvements if persevered in. Begonias, especially under the influence of hybridisation, are exceedingly "sportive" subjects, and among a goodly number of seedlings from a judicious "cross," there can scarcely fail to occur one or more breaks into a class or type superior to either of the parent plants. And the further removed from what may be termed "related" the parents are, the finer will the result prove to be, in all probability. It therefore follows that a fresh infusion of "blood," at intervals, or the importation of plants or seed from

SEED SAVING AND HYBRIDISATION.

other sources, will be beneficial, and in practice this is found to be the case, provided only that the newly imported "strain" is not in any way inferior to the stock already in hand. In large collections, where many of the individuals are far removed from one another in character and descent, this point is not of quite so much consequence as where the number of plants is limited; but even the largest collection will probably be benefited more or less by the infusion of fresh "blood" at intervals.

But in some cases, as where, for instance, it is desired to produce any particular colour or other characteristic, it is not possible to select types differing in all respects for breeding from, and what may be termed "in-breeding" must to some extent be resorted to. For instance, supposing an improved form of a white flower to be desired, it would be a very slow way of going to work to cross the best white in the stock with one of any other colour, for hardly one in fifty of the seedlings would come white, the majority of course reverting to the more natural or normal colour of red or pink. Theoretically, perhaps, such might be the best way of obtaining an improved form, and even in practice the progeny would probably possess more vigour than the result of a cross between two closely-related and more or less similar white flowers. But the shortest way to go to work is to select two plants of the same colour, or nearly so, but differing in other respects, and if possible obtained from different sources. For instance, supposing one parent to be a large but lovely-formed flower, perhaps tinged or tinted with pink, we should select for the other parent a plant bearing a well-shaped, purely white bloom, even if it were somewhat small.

Among the progeny of such a cross would be almost certain to be found one or more seedlings in which the good qualities of each of the parents were blended, to the exclusion of their faults, and thus an improvement would have been effected. Next season, starting again with these blooms, faults still remaining will be eliminated and good qualities still further developed, and thus a constant progress towards perfection is effected.

In hybridising, a good general rule is to select for the second parent a flower possessing those qualities that the first is deficient in. For instance, supposing a plant with large but rather loosely-shaped pink blooms to be taken in hand, we should select for the other plant a well-shaped—*i.e.*, circular—bloom of a red or crimson colour, with good substance and habit, and among the produce would be sure to be found at least a few plants decidedly superior to either of the parents, combining the good points of both. It does not greatly matter which way the cross is made; on the whole, perhaps, the female parent has generally more influence upon the character of the seedlings than the pollen-bearing parent, though at times we have noticed that pollen from an exceptionally fine bloom of a distinct character produced a remarkable advance in the quality and number of the seedlings produced, some of them being far superior to the female in all respects, and one or two even ahead of the male. But, as a matter of fact, there is a great deal of chance work in hybridising, especially when violent crosses (*i.e*, between widely-different individuals) are made. Any one cross, if of an experimental nature in particular, may be a great success or may turn out a failure; yet judicious selection, combined with perseverance, are bound to tell in time, and will always ensure success in the end.

If, on the other hand, any particular characteristic, such as depth or purity of colour, great size, dwarf habit, or the like be desired, then both the plants selected for parents should possess the required quality in a marked degree; and by again selecting those of the seedlings that most nearly approach the desired standard, in time something approaching perfection, or at any rate a very high degree of excellence, will be attained.

This may appear something like a contradiction of what has been said previously, but though extreme crosses are undeniably useful in their way, yet it does not do to put all our eggs in one basket and to develop any one characteristic, or to secure and bring to perfection any particular class or type of flower that may have been obtained; the surest, and, indeed, only way is to breed solely from those that already exhibit the character or tendency required in a marked degree. But the breeders should not be related, if this can be avoided, or if not, let the relationship be as distant as possible. For instance, if two of the darkest-coloured red or crimson flowers in the collection are intercrossed, they will ultimately produce a much deeper shade, though two or three, or perhaps several generations of seedlings may have to be raised before the desired result is obtained.

Again, the erect-flowering type, which is one of the most useful and effective departures that have yet occurred, was obtained simply by inter-crossing examples that showed a tendency to hold their blooms upright, and anyone with a few dozen plants to select from may attain the same result in the course of two or three years; there is also plenty of room for improvement in this class still.

It will thus be seen that any flower possessing some good points, but deficient in one or two respects, may have these faults amended—perhaps entirely eradicated in the course of a generation or two—by being crossed with another variety possessing the characteristics in which the first was wanting, and at the same time any desirable "break" or style of flower may be secured and brought to perfection by working on examples exhibiting a more or less decided tendency to the desired type.

After working among these flowers for two or three years, and having become pretty well conversant with the characteristics of the different varieties, it is surprising how many more or less distinct types are found to exist, defined not so much by colour, though this to some extent is a guide, as by the form and character of the blooms, by the habit of the plant, and some peculiarity of foliage, etc. When thoroughly at home among them, one can almost always tell with tolerable certainty the source from which any seedling possessing any noticeable characteristic was derived, without the help of tallies or numbers. Not only the plants themselves, but even the tubers, and also the seed, minute as this is, are subject to certain variations, denoting the class to which they belong. Thus the seed of double-flowering Begonias is easily distinguished by the practised eye, and the seed of (single) white and also yellow varieties presents a different appearance to that of the red flowers of various shades.

Hybridising Double Flowers.

THE hybridisation and raising of the double-flowering kinds is, if possible, an even more interesting occupation than in the case of the singles, requiring more skill and care, and presenting a still wider field for improvement and variety. The great difficulty in impregnating the double varieties is to obtain pollen of the right sort, for though female flowers are plentiful on almost any plant with double blooms, yet a thoroughly double *male* bloom produces no pollen, and if pollen from single flowers be employed, the proportion of true doubles among the resultant seedlings will be exceedingly small. The only alternative is to obtain pollen from semi-double blooms, and to this end it is necessary to select and keep in hand a stock of these for breeding purposes. It must be borne in mind that the more nearly double the pollen-producing blooms are, the larger will be the proportion of double flowers among the progeny; and also that it is very unwise to make use of pollen from any weedy third-rate blooms with only a tendency to doubleness. The pollen-bearing parent should really be, in size, substance, form, and colour as well, if possible, superior to the seed-parent, if any real advance is to be made. So that whenever among a batch of seedlings a plant is noticed bearing partly-double blooms, with bold round petals of good substance and of a clear decided colour, whatever that may be, and of a stiff dwarf habit, it should be put aside for a pollen-producer; and the female blooms on a plant with fully double flowers fertilised with such pollen will produce a large proportion—sixty or seventy per cent.—of really fine double flowers. But the *best* pollen is that at times afforded by plants which when in full vigour produce only fully double blooms; some of these when starved or past their best, and "running out," will throw a few partly-double blooms, from which a little pollen may be obtained, and this worked on the female blooms of other fine doubles will afford in some cases as much as ninety per cent. of doubles among the seedlings. But this cannot always be obtained, many of the finest varieties remaining double to the last. Starvation, and keeping the plants dry at the root in small pots, and exposed to strong sunshine, are the most effectual means for obtaining a little pollen, and as such is simply invaluable—worth many times its weight in gold—it is worth making some effort to obtain.

When impregnated mark the blooms carefully, and note the particulars of the cross. Encourage the pods to swell and ripen by maintaining a somewhat dry and very airy atmosphere, with gentle warmth, and a fair amount of sunshine acting on the plants will be found beneficial. Also do not give more than just enough water at the root to keep the plants from flagging. Damp is the great enemy of the pods when swelling and ripening, so that should the weather prove dull, a little fire heat should put on, and an abundance of air admitted in any case.

As a rule, from seed saved in the ordinary way, or such as is usually sold by trade growers, not more than fifty, or at most sixty per cent. of double flowers can be expected—often there will be less than this even. But by the exercise of great care, and the use of pollen from flowers as nearly double as possible, seventy, eighty, and even ninety per cent. of doubles may be obtained. It is strange that the first one or two blooms on seedling plants are seldom so double as those that succeed them, and also that any check, such as re-potting, will often cause the blooms to come only partly double for a time. The fact is that fully double flowers are, as a rule, only produced by a plant in full health and vigour. The finest condition is generally attained when the plant is becoming slightly pot-bound after having attained a good size, and the vigour kept up by means of frequent doses of weak liquid manure. Any single flowers produced among the doubles are usually worthless, being almost invariably poor, weak, flimsy things.

The First Double Varieties.

The race of doubles arose in the first place from a few plants that were noticed to possess rather more than the usual number of petals. These were inter-crossed, and the petals gradually became more numerous, until at last the whole of the anthers (which in true doubles are simply converted into petals) became displaced, and perfectly double blooms resulted. The first doubles of any note or degree of excellence that were sent out, were Alba plena, white; Anemonæ-flora plena, rosy red; Argus, vermilion; Gloire de Nancy, bright vermilion; Lemoinei, orange; Louis Van Houtte, orange-scarlet; Pres. Burelle, a rather bright red; Salmonea plena, salmon-rose; W. E. Gumbleton, bright salmon. These are all that were to be found in Messrs. Laing's list of 1877, and were introduced, we believe, during 1875 and 1876. Most of these, however, were only partly double, and would look very poor beside many of the introductions of the last two or three years.

The great variety of form among the double-flowering Begonias constitutes one of their great charms. Almost all are beautiful in their way, and lovely and almost perfect as many of the new varieties are, there is evidently still room for improvement in this respect—in fact, none can possibly say what these flowers are yet capable of becoming. In our opinion, the dwarf-habited erect-flowered class, with round petals, is much the most desirable and promising class, the blooms showing to so much better effect to a spectator above them (which is usually the case) than the drooping-flowered kinds can possibly do. Some beds of these dwarf erect double kinds, which we have seen in Messrs. Laing's nursery, though only seedlings, presented a most beautiful appearance, and fully confirmed our previous opinion of them. Being in the open air the growth is exceedingly short and stiff, and the flower stems very strong; and though fully exposed to every ray of sunshine, neither foliage nor flowers seem to suffer in the least, but gain an unusual degree of substance and health.

It may, perhaps, be as well to add a few words on what should almost "go without saying," viz., that all Begonias intended to produce seed must have been well hardened previously, and be exposed to plenty of sun and air. Soft and sappy or shaded plants must not be expected to seed well; in fact, they will not—cannot do it. Never mind the blooms going at the edges a little, they are of no consequence at this stage; it is the pods that we want. Keeping the plants somewhat short of water greatly tends to solidify the tissues, and this, with plenty of sun and air, will ensure pods that will neither drop, shrivel, nor "shank off." We would rather put our seedling plants out-of-doors altogether during August and September than keep them in a close, dark, or shaded house.

THE BEST FORM OF BEGONIA HOUSE.

THE best form of glasshouse in which to bloom Begonias to perfection is a span-roofed structure, in an open and sunny position, built entirely above the ground, and running east and west, or nearly so. This is obviously a better direction than north and south, because in the latter case shading must be given on both sides, and if this is done by means of blinds on rollers one must be let down early, and taken off again shortly after mid-day, while that on the west side must be drawn rather before noon, and left on till near sunset, thus rendering two blinds and double trouble necessary; whereas an east and west house only needs, if the roof is of moderate pitch, a single blind on the south side, which, with perhaps a slight sprinkle of whitewash on the north, just at. midsummer, will answer every purpose, and the plants will constantly enjoy the benefit of the full north light, even while the shading is on.

If a number of specimen plants are to be grown, and a house is set apart for them, a wide span-roofed structure, with a stage in the centre, one on each side, and two pathways, is undoubtedly the best form for not only is a wide and therefore comparatively lofty structure more suitable for the plants, but fine specimens present a much better appearance arranged on a central stage, where they are viewed from the outside, than they can possibly do on narrow side stages. There is also much more accommodation for hanging baskets in a house of this description than in a smaller and lower structure. Suitable dimensions for a house of this class would be,—centre stage, 8 feet. in width, a 3-foot pathway on each side of this, and a 3 or 4 feet wide staging again outside the path, giving a total width of 20 to 22 feet, or say 25 feet wide (outside measurement) for a fine roomy structure; the length may be anything from 30 to 100 feet or more. The stages should be about 3 feet in height, strongly made, and of open construction. Flooring boards, 1 inch thick, and 4 to 6 inches in width are perhaps better than the battens usually employed, particularly for large plants, as being stronger, cheaper, and affording better standing for the pots; a space of from 1 to 1½ inch should be left between each, to allow of a free circulation of air.

Side lights—vertical glazed sashes—of about 3 feet in height should be arranged above the level of the stages on each side; these, or at any rate every alternate one, should be hinged on to the upper plate, to act as ventilators when required, and they may be worked either by the usual arm and lever arrangement, or, if economy is an object, singly by hand, with a block and button to keep them in position. Supposing the width of the house from the outside of the wall plates to be 20 feet, the ridge-plank apex of the roof should be fixed at a distance of 7 feet 6 inches or 8 feet above the level of the upper plate or eaves of the house; this will give a good pitch.

Roof ventilators must be large and frequent, so as to allow free egress to overheated air. The wider and longer are the panes of glass employed, the stronger will the light inside the house be, and the results will prove proportionately better. We have seen houses with glass 2 feet in width, but do not think it is at all necessary to go so far as this, and if a space of 18 inches is allowed between the bars, and the panes are cut to a length of 2 feet or 2 feet 6 inches, with bars no wider than is actually necessary, and small laps, ample light for any purpose will be admitted.

Such a house could be heated by three rows of 4-inch piping along each side under the staging; or two rows on each side, and two or three up the centre of the houses, would do equally well, if not better. This would afford sufficient heat to bloom the plants nicely from April or May till nearly Christmas. Large specimens arranged on the central stage, the taller ones being elevated on inverted pots along the centre, so as to form a sloping bank towards each side, will afford a splendid effect, while the smaller plants can occupy the side stages.

Begonias of moderate size can, of course, be flowered well in a house of much smaller dimensions than the above. For a narrow house, however, a rather steeper pitched roof would be advisable—say with an inclination of 45°. For such a house, 12 feet is a very good width with a pathway 2 feet or 2 feet 6 inches wide down the centre, and open lath or board staging 2½ feet or 3 feet in height on either side. Any glass at the sides is not actually necessary, though a house so constructed looks much better than where the rafters rest directly on the wall plate, and there is also a decided gain in head-room. If side lights are provided they need not be more than 18 inches or 2 feet in height, and though with abundant roof ventilation side air is not indispensable, yet it will be as well that these should be made to open, or if there is nothing at the sides but brickwork, at least some wooden flaps or slides should be arranged at intervals along each side of the house. The only disadvantage of this class of house is that, owing to the limited head-room, the larger plants must stand towards the front of the stage, consequently hiding to a great extent the smaller ones behind, so that the effect is partially lost. A 4-inch flow and return pipe on each side beneath the staging will suffice to warm such a house thoroughly.

Some growers appear to do these Begonias very well on solid beds, surfaced with ashes or shingle. At Swanley the whole of the plants are grown thus, with the best results, but as a general rule, like Pelargoniums (Show and Regal varieties), they succeed much better on open staging, where there is a free and constant movement of the air among them. At the same time, should there be hot pipes immediately beneath such staging, and these have to be maintained at a somewhat high temperature, we should so far disregard this principle as to lay down some slates over the pipes, to prevent the heated air acting directly on the plants.

SELECT LISTS OF BEGONIAS.

SINGLE VARIETIES.

A. MAYES, rich crimson
A. W. TAIT, intense crimson
BALL OF FIRE, scarlet
BLACK DOUGLAS, carmine-crimson
CAPTAIN ROGERS, rosy crimson
CHARMER, carmine-crimson
COUNTESS OF ROSSLYN, bronze-orange
DISTINCTION, crimson, white centre
DUCHESS OF EDINBURGH, yellow, shaded orange
DUKE OF EDINBURGH, maroon, shaded chestnut
EARL OF CHESTERFIELD, vivid crimson
EARL OF ROSSLYN, orange-scarlet
E. H. WOODALL, orange-scarlet
EMILY TEESDALE, white
EXONIENSIS, orange-scarlet
F. E. LAING, velvety crimson
GOLDEN QUEEN, golden yellow
GUARDSMAN, vermilion
HER MAJESTY, blush, rose-pink centre
LADY BROOKE, rose, shaded violet
LADY CHESTERFIELD, rosy pink
LORD CREWE, violet-crimson
LORD LEWISHAM, vivid scarlet
MARCHIONESS OF BUTE, rosy pink
MARQUIS OF BUTE, carmine-crimson
MRS. BELLEW, pink
MRS. ENO, salmon, suffused with pink
MRS. LAING, white
MRS. MANDY, yellow

MRS. RAIKES, pink, shaded violet
MRS. WEEKES, white, rose-pink edge
MISS MALCOLMSON, white
MISS NEVE, salmon
MR. A. FORBES, vivid crimson
MR. COCKBURN, orange-scarlet
MR. MURPHY, pink
OUR LEADER, soft red, light centre
PINK QUEEN, light pink
PRIMROSE QUEEN, pale yellow
PRINCE ALBERT VICTOR, orange-scarlet
PRINCE OF WALES, crimson-scarlet
PRINCESS LOUISE, white
PRINCESS VICTORIA, rosy carmine, pale centre
PRINCESS OF WALES, rosy pink
PURITY, white
QUEEN VICTORIA, deep rose
RILEY SCOTT, crimson
ROSE PERFECTION, rose
SIR PETER LUMSDEN, crimson-scarlet
SIR STAFFORD NORTHCOTE, lake-red
SIR W. HART-DYKE, rich pink
SNOWFLAKE, white
STANSTEAD SURPRISE, deep crimson
STAR OF GOLD, yellow
TOREY LAING, yellow and orange
VESUVIUS, bright orange
WHITE PERFECTION, white
WILLIAM SPINKS, rose.

SELECT BEGONIAS.

BEGONIAS SUITABLE FOR BASKETS.

ANTOINETTE GUÉRIN, white, cream centre
BLANCHE DUVAL, creamy white
CLOVIS, orange-scarlet
ESTHER, crimson, rose-pink centre
FORMOSA, rosy carmine, white centre
FRANCIS BUCHNER, cerise, shaded orange
GABRIELLE LEGROS, sulphur-white
GLOIRE DE NANCY, crimson-scarlet
INCENDIE, reddish scarlet
LORD MAYOR, dark rose
LOUIS BOUCHET, orange-scarlet
MADAME ARNOULT, blush-pink
MARIE BOUCHET, reddish purple
PENDULA (Laing), deep rose
ROSAMONDE, rose-pink.

DOUBLE-FLOWERED VARIETIES.

AGNES SORREL, flesh-white
ALBA FIMBRIATA, white
ALBA MAGNA, white
ALBA ROSEA, rosy pink
ANNA, COUNTESS OF KINGSTON, salmon, yellow centre
ANTOINETTE GUÉRIN, white, creamy centre
BLANCHE DUVAL, creamy white, blush guard petals
BLANCHE JEAN PIERRE, white tint
C. FELLOWES, red, suffused crimson
CANARY BIRD, yellow
CLEMENCE DENIZARD, deep rose
CLOVIS, orange-red
COMMANDANT BASSET, soft shade of red
COMTESSE H. DE CHOISEUL, rose
DAVISII FLORE PLENO SUPERBA, crimson-scarlet
DR. DUKE, scarlet
EARL OF BESSBOROUGH, buff-yellow, red edge
ETNA, reddish scarlet
FÉLIX CROUSSE, orange-scarlet
FORMOSA, rosy carmine, white centre
GABRIELLE LEGROS, sulphur-white
GARNET, orange-scarlet
GLOIRE DE NANCY, vermilion
GLORY OF STANSTEAD, rose, white centre
GLOW-WORM, bright crimson
GOLIATH, crimson-cerise
H. LITTLE, crimson-scarlet
HERCULES, orange-scarlet
HON. MRS. PLUNKETT, salmon, with blush shade
JEAN SOUPERT, deep salmon
JUBILEE, magenta-rose
KING OF THE BEGONIAS, crimson-scarlet
KING OF THE CRIMSONS, crimson, shaded maroon
LADY HULSE, yellow
LADY LENNOX, yellow
LÉON DE ST. JEAN, reddish scarlet
LILLIE, salmon-rose
LORD BEACONSFIELD, scarlet-carmine
LORD LOUGHBOROUGH, bright scarlet
LORD MAYOR, dark rose
LORD RANDOLPH, crimson-scarlet
LOUIS BOUCHET, orange-scarlet
LOUIS D'OR, saffron-yellow
LOUISE DE GOUSSAINCOURT, light pink
MADAME ARNOULT, salmon-rose
MADAME AUGUSTE CROUET, salmon, shaded pink
MADAME COMESSE, satiny, salmon-rose
MADAME CROUSSE, flesh-rose
MADAME DE DUMAST, rose, flesh centre
MADAME DE SARGAS, soft pink, tinted salmon

MADAME E. GALLÉ, salmon, orange centre
MADAME E. PYNAERT, creamy yellow
MAJOR STUDDERT, bright red
MRS. AMY ADCOCK, salmon-red
MRS. BRISSENDEN, salmon-pink
MRS. H. G. MURRAY-STEWART, scarlet
MRS. J. L. MACFARLANE, salmon-pink
MRS. G A. PARTRIDGE, yellow
MARCHIONESS OF STAFFORD, creamy white
MARQUIS OF STAFFORD, carmine-crimson
MONS. CASSET, salmon, orange centre
M. DUVIVIER, rosy crimson
M. PAUL DE VICQ, carmine-cerise
OCTAVIE, white
PAVILLON JAUNE, yellow
PRINCE OF WALES, crimson
PRINCESS OF WALES, white
QUEEN OF DOUBLES, rosy crimson
ROBIN ADAIR, carmine-crimson
ROSAMONDE, rosy pink
ROSETTE, blush-pink
SIR GARNET, orange-scarlet
SUZANNA HATCHETTE, rosy pink
T. HEWITT, crimson-scarlet
T. MOORE, salmon-red
VIRGINALIS, pure white
WILLIAM BEALBY, deep scarlet.

NEW DOUBLE-FLOWERING BEGONIAS.
To be sent out in 1889.

Those printed in italics have received First Class Certificates.

Adonis (Laing), salmon, light centre
ARGUS (Laing), violet-rose
Camellia (Laing), rosy crimson
CARNATION (Laing), pink, edged white
Claribel (Laing), deep pink, white centre
DAVISII GIGANTEA FLORE PLENO (Laing), reddish crimson
DUCHESS OF TECK (Laing), pure yellow
Enchantress (Cannell), soft salmon
GIGANTEA (Laing), salmon-rose
GLOW (Laing), glowing scarlet
HARTINGTON (Laing), rose
H. BARNET (Laing), darkest crimson
IONA (Laing), salmon-red
LADY JULIAN GOLDSMID (Laing), bright pink
Lady Mary Fitzwilliam (Cannell), pink
LADY ROTHSCHILD (Laing), pink, white centre
LEONORA (Laing), flesh, edged with pink
LORD ROTHSCHILD (Laing), bright crimson
MAGGIE RUST (Laing), rosy pink
Marginata (Laing), white, edged pink
MRS. CARTER (Laing), delicate pink
Mrs. Midson (Cannell), white
Mrs. D. Miller (Cannell), flesh pink
MRS. G. PAUL (Cannell), pale cream
MRS. F. WILSON (Cannell), salmon-pink
Mrs. B. Wynne (Cannell), salmon
MISS BRYCESON (Cannell), pure white
Mr. H. Adcock (Laing), crimson-scarlet
Perfection (Laing) deep salmon-red
Princess Maud (Laing), white
PURITY (Cannell), white
ROSY GEM (Laing) bright rose,
Scarlet Perfection (Laing), vivid scarlet
Sir John Pender (Cannell), salmon-red
SIR JULIAN GOLDSMID, (Laing) rosy red
Snowball (Laing), white
Terra Cotta (Laing), pale red
TRIUMPH (Cannell), rich pink
Viscountess Cranbrook (Laing), bright rose, white centre
W. F. Bennett (Cannell), yellow

INDEX.

	PAGE
Arrangement of Begonias in beds	82
Autumn flowering, culture of plants for	71
Baskets, Begonias suitable for	102
Bedding-out plants, value of Begonias as	4
Bedding-out, Begonias for	79
Beds, preparing for planting	81
Begonia, Acme	21
,, Adonis	78
,, boliviensis	14
,, Camellia	89
,, Chelsoni	20
,, Clarkei	16
,, Davisii	16
,, Emperor	22
,, Felix Crousse	59
,, Frœbelii	18
,, Glow	61
,, intermedia	20
,, John Heal	76
,, Mr. Poë	45
,, Mons. Truffaut	65
,, Pearcei	14
,, Prince Henry	85
,, Princess Beatrice	85
,, Queen Victoria	26
,, ,, of Whites	22
,, rosæflora	16
,, Rosamonde	63
,, Rose Céleste	87
,, Sedeni	18
,, socotrana	74
,, Veitchii	14

	PAGE
Begonia, Virginalis	57
,, Viscountess Doneraile	21
,, White Queen	22
,, Winter Gem	78
Begonia, essential characters of the genus	10
Begonia family, a brief sketch of the	10
Begonias, arrangement of, in beds	82
,, behaviour of, under cultivation	12
,, for Bedding	79
,, double-flowering	56
,, double, erect flowering	60
,, double, hybridising	97
,, doubles, select	103
,, new varieties of	104
,, for exhibition	67
,, for late autumn flowering	71
,, history of the	14
,, how and when to fertilise	91
,, management of, in autumn	72
,, the new race of winter-flowering	74
,, on packing	69
,, properties of	86, 90
,, select lists of	102
,, suitable for baskets	102
,, as town plants	9
,, value of, for bedding-out	4
,, as wet weather plants	5

INDEX.

Entry	Page
Begonia house, best form of	100
Bull, Mr. W., hybrids raised by	24
Cannell, Mr. H., hybrids introduced and raised by	28
Characteristics, general, of Begonias; interesting exceptions to the	11
Compost for Begonias	48, 50, 62
Continental Seedlings	30
Crousse, M. Felix, hybrids raised by	30
Cuttings, propagation by	43
Double-flowering varieties	56
,, varieties, the first raised,	22, 98
Erect-flowering section	60
Exhibition, Begonias for	67
Fertilisation, artificial	95
,, natural	92
Fertilising, marking the crosses	94
Flower, treatment when in	53
Flowering, treatment after	54
Forest Hill strain, The	24
Form in double Begonias, variety of	58
Hildebrandia, the genus	13
History of the Tuberous Begonia	14
Hybrid, The first garden	18
Hybridising double Begonias	97
Hybridisation and seed saving	86
Hybrids raised by Messrs. Veitch	20
Improvements in the Begonia	3
Introducer of the Begonia	32
Laing, Mr. John, hybrids raised by	24
Leaf cuttings	45
Manures, artificial, feeding with	68
O'Brien, Mr. J., hybrids raised by	22
Packing Begonias, hints on	69
Pearce, Mr. R., the late	32
Plants, small v. large, for bedding	79
,, suitable for combination with Begonias	84
Potting, on	49, 52, 62
Pots, cultivation of Begonias in	46
Propagation of the Begonia; by Seeds, 34; by Cuttings	43
Propagating double varieties, hints on	63
Properties of single Begonias	86
,, double varieties	90
Seed saving and hybridisation	86
Seedlings, on potting on	42
,, transplanting into boxes or trays	40
,, treatment of, after germination	38
Seed pans, preparing for sowing	34
Seeds, on gathering the	94
,, propagation by	34
Selecting and starting tubers	47
,, flowers for crossing	94
Shading Begonias, on	68
Soils for Begonias	48, 50
Species of Begonia	10
Sutton & Sons, Messrs., hybrids raised by	24, 84
Swanley Collection, the	28
Temperatures for	52, 68
Treatment when in bloom	53
Tubers, selecting and starting,	47, 80
,, on preserving in winter	84
Veitch, Messrs., hybrids raised by	20
Ventilation for	52
Watering, on	48, 51, 68
Winter-flowering varieties, new race of	74

ADVERTISEMENTS.

Under Royal  Patronage.

JOHN LAING & SONS,
Seed, Bulb, and Plant Merchants,
ROSE, FRUIT-TREE, & VINE GROWERS,
FOREST HILL, LONDON, S.E.

LAING'S BEGONIAS
☞ AWARDED FOUR GOLD MEDALS.

A GREAT SPECIALITY.		A GREAT SPECIALITY.

Awarded the only JUBILEE GOLD MEDAL offered.

The Head of our Firm has made the BEGONIAS what they now are; we therefore strongly recommend purchasers to send to us DIRECT, to procure the BEST, and OUR greatly improved varieties. We only supply Seeds (Single and Double) in OUR own sealed packets, *without* which none are genuine.

No one should fail to see our GRAND FLORAL DISPLAY OF BEGONIAS during the summer months. The magnitude and quality of our collection is unapproached.

WE HAVE A GRAND STOCK OF
ORCHIDS, STOVE AND GREENHOUSE PLANTS,
Chrysanthemums, Herbaceous Plants, Florists' Flowers,
AND
➤ GENERAL ✦ OUT-DOOR ✦ NURSERY ✦ STOCK, ✦ &c. ◄
GENUINE SEEDS AND BULBS.

Best route to reach our (four) Nurseries is from Charing Cross, Cannon Street, or London Bridge (thirty minutes' ride) to Catford Bridge Station, thence a walk of five minutes; or to Forest Hill from Victoria, Kensington, and West End.

DESCRIPTIVE CATALOGUES POST FREE.

Registered Telegraphic Address—CALADIUM, LONDON.

BEGONIAS.

We have the finest and most complete collection in the world, and to confirm this statement we were awarded the first Gold Medal, and also the First Prize at the recent Show in London, open to all comers.

Daily Chronicle, 21st June, 1888.—" *Begonias.—Mr. Cannell a grand First."*—(7 entries)

Mr. J. W. TAYLOR, 81, Ann Street, Dundee, *October, 21st,* 1887.

"I gained the first prize with your Single Begonias, both at the Downfield and Dundee Shows, and there was not one at either that came within 3 inches of the size of my flowers. I have taken first prize from all the amateurs for three years. I was also first for Bronze Pelargoniums and Fuchsias, with sorts obtained from you. My collection of Begonias from you make a show in themselves, and it is the talk of the country. Some gardeners, who have a good collection themselves, came a great distance to see them, but all admitted they had nothing to be compared with mine."

Come and See.

Our fine display during the summer in eight 100-feet houses, and an acre out in the grounds, consisting of hundreds of thousands. Send for our Floral Guide, the finest illustrated and descriptive Catalogue, containing all particulars of the culture of the above, and other innumerable secrets of cultivation; sent post free.

H. CANNELL & SONS,
THE HOME OF FLOWERS,

VEITCH'S
CHOICE FLOWER SEEDS
THE FINEST IN CULTIVATION.

BEGONIA, VEITCH'S CHOICEST HYBRID.
Saved from the very finest and newest hybrids, and is undoubtedly the best strain yet offered. Per packet, 1s. 6d.

DOUBLE BEGONIA, CHOICEST HYBRID.
Saved from an unequalled collection, and may be expected to produce a large proportion of well-formed, perfectly double flowers. Per packet, 2s. 6d.

AMARYLLIS, VEITCH'S HYBRID.
Saved from the magnificent collection grown at our Chelsea Nursery. Per packet, 2s. 6d.

CALCEOLARIA, INTERNATIONAL PRIZE.
Unsurpassed for size, shape, and substance of flowers. Per packet, 2s. 6d.

CARNATION, VEITCH'S FINEST DOUBLE.
Saved from our unequalled collection of all the finest varieties; likely to produce many new beautiful sorts. Per packet, 2s. 6d.

CINERARIA, VEITCH'S SUPERB STRAIN.
Splendid large flowers, of fine form and substance. Per packet, 2s. 6d.

GLOXINIA, VEITCH'S SUPERB STRAIN.
Saved from the magnificent collection grown at our Chelsea Nursery. Per packet, 2s. 6d.

MIGNONETTE, CRIMSON KING.
A new, distinct, and most desirable variety for pot culture, throwing up numerous stout flower-stalks, terminated by extremely broad spikes of delightfully scented bright red flowers. Per packet, 1s.

NEW PRIMULA, SNOWFLAKE.
First Class Certificate Royal Horticultural Society, 1887.

The finest pure white fern-leaved variety. Flowers large, of fine form, massive substance, and exquisitely fimbriated at edge, well displayed above the dark green beautifully curled foliage. Per packet, 3s. 6d.

PRIMULAS, VEITCH'S SUPERB STRAIN.
FINEST FRINGED, RED, WHITE, AND MIXED.

These are the finest in cultivation, and were awarded a First Class Certificate by the Royal Horticultural Society for superior quality. Per packet, 2s. 6d.

☞ For full description of the above and other Choice Novelties and Specialities, see SEED CATALOGUE, forwarded Gratis and Post-free on application.

JAMES VEITCH & SONS,
ROYAL EXOTIC NURSERY, CHELSEA, LONDON, S.W.

For Garden and Greenhouse.

BARR'S SELECTED BULBS.

The Finest of 1888 Crop.

 Direct from the most reliable Bulb Farms in Holland and France.

Full Descriptive Bulb Catalogue Free on application.

FULLY ILLUSTRATED & DESCRIPTIVE DAFFODIL CATALOGUE FREE ON APPLICATION.

BARR & SON, 12 & 13, KING-ST., COVENT GARDEN, W.C.

SPECIALITIES.

ROSES, DAHLIAS, VERBENAS,
Chrysanthemums & Vines.

CATALOGUE GRATIS.

KEYNES, WILLIAMS AND CO.,
The Nurseries,
SALISBURY.

OWEN'S "IMPERIAL" BEGONIAS.

New and distinct strain, possessing a greater variety of colour than any other strain; the result of 15 years' labour. Habit dwarf and vigorous, flower stems erect, blooms of great size and substance.

AWARDED MANY CERTIFICATES AND PRIZES.

TESTIMONIAL.

July 3rd, 1888, Cambridge.

I am very pleased with the Begonias you sent me. The habit of the plants is very dwarf, flower stems erect, the flowers looking one in the face as if not ashamed to be seen.

HENRY RIDGEWELL.

TUBERS AND SEED BY POST.

CHRYSANTHEMUMS.

The finest collection in the kingdom; 1,200 varieties, warranted true to name.

Descriptive and priced Catalogue, with cultural directions by E. Molyneux and C. Orchard, 6d., free to purchasers.

PLANTS AND CUTTINGS BY POST.

ROBERT OWEN,
FLORAL NURSERY,
MAIDENHEAD.

⇢BEGONIAS⇠

THE LARGEST AND BEST COLLECTION IN THE WEST OF ENGLAND.

CULTIVATED BY

B. R. DAVIS,

The Yeovil Nurseries,

YEOVIL, SOMERSET.

BEGONIAS for Exhibition.
BEGONIAS for Conservatory and Greenhouse.
BEGONIAS for Window and Table Decoration.
BEGONIAS for Bedding Out.
BEGONIAS, Double, Named, and Unnamed.
BEGONIAS, Single, to Name, Colour, or Mixed.
Inspection of **BEGONIAS** invited during July, August, & September.
BEGONIAS in immense quantities.

Descriptive Catalogue Free on application to

B. R. DAVIS,

THE YEOVIL NURSERIES, YEOVIL, SOMERSET.

A REVISED AND ENLARGED CHEAP EDITION

OF

VINES & VINE CULTURE

"The most complete and exhaustive Treatise on Grapes ever published."

BY

ARCHIBALD F. BARRON,

Superintendent of the Royal Horticultural Society's Gardens, Chiswick;
Secretary of the Fruit Committee; Author of British Apples, Pears, &c.

COPIOUSLY ILLUSTRATED.

Demy 8vo. Handsomely Bound in Cloth, price 5s.; Post Free, 5s. 6d.

A. F. BARRON,

13, SUTTON COURT ROAD, CHISWICK, LONDON.

ADVERTISEMENTS. vii

☞ *None is Genuine that does not bear our Name on the Sack.*

THOMSON'S
IMPROVED
Vine, Plant & Vegetable Manure

AWARDED ONLY MEDAL	—FOR—	ARTIFICIAL MANURES AT Edinburgh International Exhibition, 1886.

This Manure, on its own merits, has come rapidly into extensive use. The materials it is composed of are of the highest manurial value, and so balanced as to combine immediate with lasting effects. It is a safe and certain Manure for every fruit-bearing plant from the Vine downwards, as well as for Pot Plants and Vegetables.

—TERMS—

1 ton	... £18 0 0	1 cwt.	... £1 0 0	7 lb. tins	...	£0 3 6
10 cwts.	... 9 10 0	56 lbs.	... 0 10 0	3 ,,	...	0 2 0
5 ,,	... 5 0 0	28 ,,	... 0 6 0	1 ,,	...	0 1 0

Directions for use are placed in each Sack, and printed on the Tins.

Orders of and above 1 cwt. Carriage Paid to all Stations. Can be had of all Nurserymen and Seedsmen.

Agent for London:—
Mr. JAMES GEORGE,
10, Victoria Road, Putney.

Sole Agent for Channel Islands:—
Mr. J. H. PARSONS,
Market Place, Guernsey.

REFERENCES CAN BE MADE TO

Mr. JONES, Royal Gardens, Windsor Castle
Mr. HENDERSON, Thoresby Park, Nottingham
Mr. MURRAY, Culzean Castle, Maybole
Mr. LYON, Ossington Hall, Nottingham
Mr. BAILLIE, Luton Hoo, Luton
Mr. GOUGH, Harefield Grove, Uxbridge
Mr. M'INDOE, Hutton Hall, Yorkshire
Mr. BURNETT, Deepdene, Dorking
Mr. M'INTYRE, The Glen, Innerleithen
Mr. GEORGE MUNRO, Covent Garden, London
H. PIGGOTT, Esq., Tunbridge Wells
Mr. LAING, Salisbury Green, Edinburgh

Mr. CROSSART, Oswald House, Oswald Road, Edinburgh
Mr. KAY, Long Lane Nursery, Finchley, N.
Mr. MACKENZIE, Eriska, Oban
Mr. M'LEOD, Brentham Park, Stirling
Mr. TEMPLE, Carron House, Falkirk
Mr. JOHN BAYNE, Patshull Grdns, Wolverhampton
Mr. MURRAY, The Gardens, Park Hall, Polmont, N.B.
Mr. J. WITHERSPOON, Red Rose Vineries, Chester-le-Street

And many others.

SOLE MAKERS:—

Wm. Thomson & Sons, Tweed Vineyard, Clovenfords, Galashiels.

✦ ORCHIDS ✦

WM. THOMSON & SONS have a very Large Stock of HIGH-CLASS ORCHIDS, which they are prepared to offer on very reasonable terms. These may be had on application.

THE GARDENING WORLD.

ESTABLISHED 1884.

The Largest and Best Penny Weekly Gardening Paper.

PUBLISHED EVERY FRIDAY—PRICE ONE PENNY,

AND CONTAINS

WELL-WRITTEN & INSTRUCTIVE ARTICLES

ON THE CULTURE OF

ALL USEFUL FRUITS, FLOWERS, AND VEGETABLES.

THE CURRENT WORK OF THE GARDEN.

ORCHID NOTES AND GLEANINGS.

WEEKLY LETTERS ON

GARDENING IN SCOTLAND AND IRELAND.

SPECIAL CONTRIBUTIONS ON

Florists' Flowers AND the Amateurs' Garden.

NOTICES OF NEW BOOKS—REPORTS OF FLOWER SHOWS.

THE HORTICULTURAL NEWS OF THE WEEK,

AND

Illustrations by the best Artists.

A FIRST-CLASS MEDIUM FOR ADVERTISING.

From all Newsagents and Booksellers, or direct from the Office for 6s. 6d. per annum, PREPAID.
Foreign Subscription to all Countries in the Postal Union, 8s. 8d. *per annum.*

VOLUMES I. TO IV., HANDSOMELY BOUND, 6s. 6D. EACH.

Postal and Money Orders should be made payable to B. WYNNE, at Drury Lane.

PUBLISHING OFFICE :—

17, CATHERINE STREET, COVENT GARDEN, LONDON, W.C.

The National Chrysanthemum Society.

Programme of Arrangements for 1888.

ROYAL AQUARIUM, WESTMINSTER.

GRAND EXHIBITION,
SEPTEMBER 12th and 13th,
CHRYSANTHEMUMS & DAHLIAS.

THE
Chrysanthemum Exhibition & Fête
NOVEMBER 7th and 8th.

MID-WINTER SHOW,
JANUARY 9th and 10th, 1889.
CHRYSANTHEMUMS, CYCLAMENS, PRIMULAS, &c.

FLORAL COMMITTEE MEETINGS
SEP. 12th, OCT. 10th and 24th, NOV. 7th and 21st, DEC. 5th, and JAN. 9th, 1889.

(All persons, whether Members of the Society or not, are invited to exhibit at the Floral Meetings.)

THE
GRAND PROVINCIAL SHOW
WILL BE HELD IN THE
CORN EXCHANGE, SHEFFIELD,
NOVEMBER 16th and 17th.

Schedules and all particulars sent on application to
Mr. WILLIAM HOLMES,
Frampton Park Nurseries, Hackney.

Members of the Society are entitled to a pass for every Show.
Annual Subscription of Members, 5s.; of Fellows, 21s.

F. SANDER & CO.,
ST. ALBANS.

LARGEST AND FINEST STOCK

OF

ESTABLISHED ORCHIDS

IN THE KINGDOM.

WE HAVE A MAGNIFICENT COLLECTION
OF ALL THE
BEST NAMED
DOUBLE AND SINGLE BEGONIAS,
THE FORMER MOSTLY BY CONTINENTAL GROWERS,
AND

We confidently assert that Double Begonias sent out by French Raisers are far in advance of any English Strain.

WE ALSO CULTIVATE A FINE LOT OF LARGE-FLOWERED SINGLES.

Our prices will be found extremely reasonable on comparison with other well-known firms.

DESCRIPTIVE LIST FREE ON APPLICATION.

MORLEY & Co.,
EXOTIC NURSERIES,
PRESTON, LANCASHIRE.

ADVERTISEMENTS.

CONTRACTORS TO HER MAJESTY'S WAR DEPARTMENT.

THE THAMES BANK IRON COMPANY.

GOLD MEDAL, BIRMINGHAM, 1872.

GOLD AND SILVER MEDALS, LONDON, 1883 & 1886.

(TELEGRAPHIC ADDRESS—HOT WATER, LONDON.—TELEPHONE—No. 4763.)

ORIGINAL MANUFACTURERS of this CLASS of BOILER.

Supplied in several sizes for the last Thirty-five Years to the leading Horticulturists.

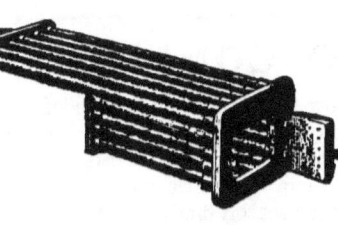

Several improvements have from time to time been introduced, including Water Bars, Furnace Door hung upon the front of Boiler, &c., as shown in illustration, thus making it complete in itself.

There has been a great demand for this Boiler, and the success attending it has been general.

The largest and most complete Stock of

HOT-WATER BOILERS OF EVERY DESCRIPTION,

PIPES, CONNECTIONS, VALVES, VENTILATING GEAR, &c.,

AND INVITE INSPECTION OF SAME.

Price List on application, Free.   Illustrated Catalogue, One Shilling.

UPPER GROUND STREET,
BLACKFRIARS, S.E.

ORCHIDS A SPECIALTY.

The stock at the Clapton Nursery is of such magnitude, that without seeing it, it is not easy to form an adequate conception of its unprecedented extent.

ROSES, FRUIT TREES, VINES, ORNAMENTAL-LEAVED and FLOWERING PLANTS in variety, and of fine quality.

The glass structures cover an area of 297,300 *feet. Inspection invited.*

HUGH LOW & CO.,
CLAPTON NURSERY, LONDON;
AND
BUSH HILL PARK NURSERY, ENFIELD.

TO COMPETITORS.

OUR House is now the recognised source of many of the most reliable strains of Flowers and Vegetables in the Market. Ever since its foundation we have made the requirements of Exhibitors and Competitors our special study, and our Specialties have become so firmly established in public favour that every season marks a considerable increase in the demand for them.

SPECIALTIES.

Flowers.	Vegetables.
PANSIES	LEEKS
DAHLIAS	PARSLEY
PHLOXES	PARSNIPS
ROSES	TURNIPS
MARIGOLDS	BEETROOT
CARNATIONS	ONIONS
ASTERS, &c.	CELERY, &c.

Our Descriptive Catalogue and Competitor's Guide, extending to over 100 *pages, will be sent Gratis and Post Free to all who apply for it.*

DOBBIE & Co., Seed Growers & Florists, Rothesay, Scotland.

www.ingramcontent.com/pod-product-compliance
Lightning Source LLC
Chambersburg PA
CBHW022140160426
43197CB00009B/1368